Marina Roveda - Simone Gabrielli

LAW OF ATTRACTION TAROT

how to achieve your desires

Marina Roveda
Artwork by Simone Gabrielli

Law of Attraction Tarot

Graphics and layout: Lo Scarabeo
Cover image by Simone Gabrielli
Set edition cover image by Marta Dahlig
Traslation by Jessica Noach
Editing by Barbara Moore

© 2011 by Lo Scarabeo.
Via Cigna 110 - 10155 - Torino - Italy
info@loscarabeo.com - www.loscarabeo.com

First edition: 2011
Printed by CT Printing

Index

Introduction

All of us, at some point in our lives, have wished for something. We have felt some kind of desire or dream. Some of us go on to realize those dreams. Others give up from lack of initiative. Some never begin due to a lack of self-confidence. Some are overcome by fears. Often these self-created realities are then chalked up to bad luck.

But just what is a desire, a wish? It's an aspiration towards what you need and what you feel is missing. Desiring is part of human nature, and often helps us improve our quality of life. It's also the beginning of

THE ACT OF WISHING IS FULL OF RICHES AND JOYS OF EVERY KIND

something, because once you decide to achieve your desires, you begin connecting to a powerful current that may take you places you never dreamed of when you began your journey.

Often we feel the desire to renew ourselves, and we set ourselves goals in the hope that they will help us change for the better. But we don't always succeed in reaching our objectives, perhaps because the method we choose is inadequate, or because the objectives aren't really in line with our deepest aspirations.

What many of us don't realize, however, is that the act of wishing is not only full of riches and joys of every kind but also the desire to enjoy these blessings. It's a shame that most of us do everything in our power to protect ourselves from desiring good things, either out of

WE SET OURSELVES GOALS IN HOPE THAT THEY WILL HELP US CHANGE FOR THE BETTER

pride, fear, or love of the status quo. Many people don't even know how to dream or to wish for something, and even fewer are even conscious of what their dreams are.

Fortunately, those who have a rich inner life or are highly evolved spiritually are aware of this art because they are capable of distinguishing between real desires – the true and authentic ones – and those imposed by circumstance and those around us.

Asking the questions what do I want? What makes me happy? What do I really enjoy? and searching for those answers is soulful work and the beginning of authentic desiring and wishing.

In addition to deeper self-understanding, those who know how to desire retain more control over their lives. They are convinced that when we want something, the whole universe conspires in our favor.

Those who know how to dream are not afraid to think big or to act boldly. In hard times, they are not deterred by setbacks nor do they anxiously wait for a more auspicious moment. They feed their dreams continually, knowing that the

THOSE WHO KNOW HOW TO DREAM ARE NOT AFRAID TO THINK BIG OR TO ACT BOLDLY

right conditions needed to manifest their desired reality will present themselves sooner or later. Because dreamers are confident of the outcome, they invest themselves in their dreams in every way.

Ultimately, realizing our dreams, the true and authentic desires of our soul, is the only duty we have. To succeed we need to follow the signs, embark on the journey, and remain firm in our convictions.

This is the only way to discover who we really are.
Then sharing the magic found on our journey will be child's play.

The origin of the Law of Attraction

The **Law of Attraction** is an ancient concept that was popularized by Rhonda Byrne's worldwide bestselling book *The Secret*. The book's success led to countless articles and texts on the subject, and consequently its notoriety and appeal has spread to an ever-growing audience.

According to this Law, when we desire something strongly, our wish will come true as if by magic; the Universe helps us to achieve our desires, as we draw into our lives the most favorable conditions for manifesting our dreams.

In the gospels Jesus seems to be aware of its existence when he says:

For verily I say unto you, That whosoever shall say unto this mountain, Be thou removed, and be thou cast into the sea; and shall not doubt in his heart, but shall believe that those things which he saith shall come to pass; he shall have whatsoever he saith.
[Mark 11.23]

According to these words, we need only to wholeheartedly pursue our goal, spiritually commit to the task, work hard, and give thanks to the universe with heartfelt gratitude. Hence, each of us is in a position to lead the life we wish, to achieve the goals we aspire, to and to find that which we seek.

But what are the origins of the Law of Attraction?
Sources indicate that it was in fact a secret known to Egyptian and Babylonian priests, Hindu gurus, sages of antiquity including Plato and Pythagoras, the masters of esoteric traditions and the connoisseurs of secret societies such as the Illuminati and the Masons.

A POTENTIAL THAT EXISTS IN US ALL, UNEXPRESSED AND NOT FULLY UNDERSTOOD

This concept alludes to ancient potential that exists in us all unexpressed and not fully understood. This potential can bring the abundance that characterizes the universe. We are able to use and understand this because the "secret" is part of us, hardwired into our brain. We can use it to influence reality.

A TREMENDOUSLY POWERFUL FORCE THAT CONSTANTLY INFLUENCES US

If this is true, why then are there people who turn their dreams into reality while others fail to do so? How do we recognize the most efficient strategies, the steps that consistently yield results? What is the secret of the "secret"? The concepts of the Law of Attraction can supply us with all the answers to manifesting our dreams, although those answers vary according to the objectives we are attempting to achieve.

According to Brian Tracy, internationally renowned authority on developing human potential and personal effectiveness: "*We are a living magnet; we attract in our lives people and circumstances that harmonize with our dominant thoughts*".

Anthony Robbins, one of the most famous personal development coaches talks about the "reticular activating system" or RAS, referring to the notion that when the human brain is focused on a particular goal, it will automatically notice events, people, or discussions associated with that goal.

Deepak Chopra, the endocrinologist who paved new ways to free the incredible potential that lies within each of us, talks about "coincidences." These, he says, are actually signals from

RECOGNIZING THIS CONNECTION ALLOWS US TO BE MORE AWARE AND TO LIVE A MORE FULFILLING LIFE the Universe that guide us toward that place where miracles occur. In that place we can achieve that which we each promised ourselves to achieve in life and know our true path that connects with the sphere of infinite possibilities yet to be realized.

In the end, the Law of Attraction is a tremendously powerful force that constantly influences us. To understand it means achieving a profound global vision of the links between personal reality, love, relationships and our self-awareness--because nothing happens by chance.

Therefore those people and situations that cross our path always have a reason for doing so. "Luck" or "misfortune" play no role. Rather, everything depends on the Law of Attraction. We all swim in the same sea and ride the same waves, ever conscious of who is beside us. Indeed, we are not islands but are bound together much more than we think. Recognizing this allows us to be more aware and to live a more fulfilling life.

Why consult the Law of Attraction Tarot

The Law of Attraction emphasizes the fact that the more we concentrate on something, the closer, more tangible and attainable that something becomes.

But how do we put it into practice? Can we do something to help the Universe to turn our dreams into reality?

THE MORE WE CONCENTRATE ON SOMETHING, THE CLOSER THAT SOMETHING BECOMES

If we wish to have a clear direction to follow, we must first know where we want to go. The purpose of the Law of Attraction Tarot is just that. Those who consult it can transform a dream into a tangible and attainable goal, starting with a clear understanding of the present, i.e. the situation in which one finds oneself, and arriving at the desired future.

For over 35 years, Neuro-Linguistic Programming (NLP) has studied human excellence, identifying the most effective psychophysical methods for focusing on objectives, increasing self-esteem and improving relationships and contains precise guidelines for properly formulating what we want. First and foremost, a desire must be expressed using positive language. For example, if we no longer wish to be single, we mustn't say, "I don't want to be alone anymore" since the emphasis is on that which we "don't want to be" instead of that which we "want to be." A better way to express this desire would be to say, "I want to have a meaningful relationship."

By establishing the present situation and the desired future through positive verbalization and consulting the Law of Attraction Tarot, we can then chart a course to follow, including practical actions to take.

· · · · ·

CURRENT STATE
Single

· · · · ·

DESIRED STATE
Find a romantic partner

· · · · ·

STRATEGY TO IMPLEMENT
TO LEAVE THE CURRENT STATE
AND ARRIVE AT THE DESIRED STATE
*Socialize as much as possible,
network,
frequent new places*

· · · · ·

By doing this you learn to combine action and strategy to achieve your goals faster and more efficiently. Having such knowledge allows us to be ready to take advantage of all opportunities that come our way.

In the example, having a strategy to meet new people will make us more courageous, more open, and more attractive, increasing the possibility that a seemingly chance encounter will lead to something more.

Living in this manner implies that our destiny is not a sword of Damocles hanging over our head. But rather, the path of our life is something we co-create using our creative ability and free will.

Life should be experienced as a path that lies ahead of us that includes our aspirations and satisfaction. We can give ten, forty or one hundred percent of ourselves to expressing our potential and broadening our awareness and possibly taking a quantum leap in our consciousness and our way of life.

While we should not allow ourselves to be guided by it as if it were a lifeline or a doctor, the Tarot can help us. By relying on the Tarot's rich symbolic fabric, full of numbers, symbols and energies, we can trigger our sensitivity and insight and accept the idea that the future is only one of many possible developments of our present.

Having done this, meaningful coincidences will abound in our lives and everything will change.

How to put into practice the Law of Attraction

To effectively work with the Law of Attraction, have a clear idea of your desired state. Knowing beforehand what you want to acquire or achieve avoids wasting time and energy pursuing things that don't truly match your values and objectives.

THE CHANGE MUST BE MOTIVATED
BY A REAL NEED

To succeed in this intention, the change must be motivated by a real need. You must feel a strong desire to achieve something or be experiencing a discomfort to overcome. Without a stimulating factor it is difficult to generate enough energy to set the wheels in motion.

This is not as easy as it seems, since no school teaches how to imagine your future and formulate your desires correctly, but we will try to fill this gap.

Most people find that it is extremely useful to put your wishes on paper. It is important to keep in mind the following criteria:

• *the wish must be positive*
That means eliminating the word "not" and negatively worded statements. Sentences like, "I don't wish to do this job anymore" or "I no longer want to live in that neighborhood" or "I don't wish to work for such low wages" are defined linguistically as *negative commands*. They transmit the opposite message of that which is actually desired. Therefore we have to express that which we want to be or to do (e.g. "I want to become a successful architect" or "I want to take a trip to India"), rather than what we no longer wish to be or do. These positive expressions focus on the desired reality and put less emphasis on reality we wish to leave.

While expressing our wishes it is useful to be able to answer certain questions as precisely as possible. For example, "What do I really want? By when do I want it fulfill it? Why would I like to achieve this? With whom do I want to accomplish this?" This knowledge helps us form a clearer picture of our wish, making it easier to attract it into our lives.

• the wish must be responsible

Whoever makes a wish must be able to assume full responsibility for it. The first thing you need to ask is, "Do I have the means to achieve it? Does it depend on me? What resources are at my disposal to realize my dream?" In this regard it is very important the resources be ours, not of others, and that we be able to take advantage of them.

For example, if I declare that "I want to become a world famous singer within three years," would I have the necessary means to accomplish it? I don't think so because I've never taken voice lessons. I have never performed in front of an audience, so I have no experience in the field. My love of music is not enough.

Another example would be, if I wished to marry Colin Farrell. This wish wouldn't depend solely on me but on another person, therefore I could never assume complete responsibility.

The key to expressing responsible wishes is to formulate desires that are in line with who we are, and omitting those that are impossible (for example "I would like to be 7 feet tall"), those that depend exclusively on chance (such as "I would like to win the Lottery Super Jackpot"), or those that do not depend on us but on others (like, "I wish my spouse were more punctual").

Finally, it's important to avoid confusing or ambiguous wishes, such as, "I would like to feel better." It is best to formulate clear and specific wishes like, "I would like to increase my salary by $500 a month" or "I wish to rid myself of the insomnia that is tormenting me."

• the wish must be measurable

A wish is *measurable* when there is a way to know when it has been achieved. By establishing a clear picture of exactly what we want and a way to know when we've achieved it, it becomes much simpler to achieve results.

Imagine we want to move: in this case we need to establish the timeframe in which we intend to find a new home, describing in as much detail as possible what we're looking for (for example, "I want to move to a larger apartment with more light that is close to the train station for easier commutes" is a well-formulated goal as opposed to the more generic, "I want to move").

If we set ourselves more complex goals, such as changing jobs, and fail to define them in enough detail, it will be difficult to succeed. Our brains are designed to follow specific and precise commands. That is why we need to specify the time frame and steps to take. Once these details are in place our brains, having very clear directions, can focus on what we want.

Finally, we must be absolutely convinced that we actually really want what we claim to wish for, keeping in mind the possible advantages and disadvantages. If not, we risk never reaching our goals because we will sabotage them.

• *the wish must be ecological*
In NLP, the term *ecological* doesn't refer to the safeguarding of the environment but rather being in accordance with our values and our identity. If achieving our goal means putting our health at risk, violating our principles, or compromising our relationship with our partner, then we must reflect on our choice of goal and express a desire that is perhaps more in line with who we are and our lifestyle.

If we fail to do so, we shouldn't be surprised if more than one problem arises in making our dream a reality. If, on a subconscious level we do not really approve of what we are doing, problems will surface to remind us that we are not being truthful with ourselves.

- *a wish must have at least three options in order to come true*

Last but not least, we must know of several options available to us in terms of achieving our goal or imagine several different paths to get there. NLP states that you need at least three options. One option is no choice at all. Two options is a dilemma and therefore problematic. Three options greatly improve our chances to succeed at the goals we have set since, if we fail in one approach we can try another and even another.

John Templeton, a famous American-born British business-man and philanthropist, stated that achieving a goal may take several attempts. Each attempt may bring us closer to attaining our objective, allowing us in the course of this process to express new desires.

The options are actually our inner voice that urges us on, "If at first you don't succeed, try another path."

For example, if our dream is to publish a novel but we can't find seem to find a publisher, we can take a different path to reach our goal. Entering a literary contest, contacting an agent, or simply changing the way in which we submit our manuscript by sending, instead of the usual cover letter and a synopsis of the work, perhaps a more detailed summary as well as self addressed stamped envelope to make it simpler for the publisher to get back to you.

This is why options can mean the difference between success and defeat.

To properly formulate a wish

- Understand what you really want
- Define the wish in clear detail
- Express your wish in a positive way
- Write it down
- Establish a quantifiable measure of success
- Be sure to respect your values and who you are
- Make the wish responsible
- Identify at least three paths to achieve it

How to approach the Tarot of Attraction

• It is important to treat the Law of Attraction with great respect, just as we would our dreams.

• Whenever we handle the cards in order to do a reading, it is important to clear our mind of any thoughts that might affect us negatively. This is the only way to find our inner sanctum, strengthen our self-esteem, and achieve the necessary balance to act.

Treat the Law of Attraction Tarot with great respect, just as you would your dreams

It is true that consulting the Tarot helps us to know which path will help us to grow and mature. However, it is up to us to face the wide range of possible futures, roll up our sleeves, and make sure the most favorable one becomes our reality.

The Tarot is not a magical instrument that will effortlessly solve our problems, but a tool that helps reveal our best selves, that which is capable of handling and overcoming challenges, and ultimately manifesting our wishes.

• Another necessary attitude essential for using the Tarot successfully is to have complete faith in the cards. Consulting the cards means risking an unwelcome response, exploring unknown terrains, and facing uncertainty in terms of their reliability. It is important to keep in mind that the uncertainty is an essential element of this decision-making process as it allows us to determine whether or not our desire and our need for change are indeed real. Without it, we would not be capable of knowing whether our desire for transformation is based in reality or not.

FIND OUR INNER SANCTUM,

STRENGTHEN OUR SELF-ESTEEM,

AND ACHIEVE THE NECESSARY BALANCE TO ACT

• If you feel tired, upset, or depressed you should put off consulting the cards. Surely the reading can wait a few days. It is also wise to avoid a reading if you are aware of any disturbances, including psychological ones such as feelings of skepticism about the expressed wish. These disturbances may come from you (as the person reading the cards) or the person you are reading for.

• Use the Tarot in a quiet and calm environment where it is possible for you (and the querent, if you are reading the cards for someone else) to reach a state of tranquility and relaxation. This helps you more easily to access your intuitive abilities and your sensitivity. Don't rush to write down your notes on the cards and your interpretation – take the time to reflect on the cards and their deeper meanings.

Major Arcana

The Major Arcana cards are specific symbols. They illustrate a true path to free yourself from material bonds, to achieve a higher understanding of yourself, and to see things from a new perspective. Understanding the Major Arcana often proves to be an effective means of self-care by nourishing the mind and exploring your potential and limitations. Looking at the cards one by one we will see what each Major Arcana card suggests even without having to ask a question.

The sequence of the Major Arcana

Read together, the Major Arcana cards of the Law of Attraction Tarot indicate the path each person must follow for both self-realization and achieving goal(s). The journey begins with the Fool, which symbolizes confusion—the state we find ourselves in before we have clarified our wishes.

As we create our wishes, face the challenges in manifesting them and accepting the changes they brings to our lives, we will travel through all the cards of the Major Arcana, arriving at least at The World, a card symbolizing the achievement of our goals.

Some cards are considered "active" – that is, they represent the need to act and to put ourselves on a practical plane. Others are considered "passive" – they represent the need to perceive, understand, or reflect. The active cards will be marked in green. Cards that invite introspection will be marked in blue. Two cards, Confusion (The Fool) and Fulfillment (The World), are both active and passive.

Confusion
(0 – The Fool)
When clarity is lacking and one is overwhelmed by emotions, one must learn to create inner calm and channel one's energies constructively.

Planning
(I – The Magician)
Moving freely with the mind leads to
making choices and inevitably transforms
dreams into projects

Wisdom
(II – The High Priestess)
Inspiration comes from within us,
but this does not mean to close
oneself in solitude.

Formulation
(III – The Empress)
Formulating a wish is a voluntary act;
conscious and strong.

Inner Maturity
(IV – The Emperor)
Independence, be it economic,
spiritual or emotional,
is the heart of one's identity.

Coherence
(V – The Pope)
The deepest desires are born from harmony
with oneself and not from passing whims
or external conditioning.

The Law of Attraction
(VI – The Lovers)
The ideal and the real are comparable
and attract each other, but are rarely the same thing.

Dynamism
(VII – The Chariot)
We must act and ride the current of life with joy.

Discipline
(VIII – Justice)
Sacrifice and perseverance light the path to achievement.

Concentration
(IX – The Hermit)
Patience and waiting are effective antidotes
for instability and distraction.

The Wheel of Life
(X – The Wheel of Fortune)
You should throw yourself in the game of life,
even if everything that begins sooner or later must end.

Self Confidence
(XI – Strength)
Strength is safety and stability,
not violence or misuse of power.
You compete against yourself, not others.

Doubt
(XII – The Hanged Man)
Doubt is the seed of one's conscience.
It must be understood and not feared.

Change
(XIII – Death)
Growth is change. Only that which changes
remains faithful to itself.

Reflection
(XIV – Temperance)
We must seek balance between various opposites
and conflicting desires. This is not instantaneous;
rather a slow process that happens
gradually, day after day.

Contrast
(XV – The Devil)
Some things must be confronted.

Defeat
(XVI – The Tower)
A defeat helps check our pride and readjust
our vision so we needn't start over completely.

Optimism
(XVII – The Stars)
We must find our place in the world,
wait for the right moment,
and build opportunities.

Negative Thoughts
(XVIII – The Moon)
We mustn't fear our dark side
but rather accept it
without being dominated by it.

Success
(XIX – The Sun)
We need to confront our successes in order
to grow and not stop short
of realizing our dreams.

The Renewal
(XX – Judgment)
Each end must have a corresponding beginning.

The Accomplishment
(XXI – The World)
This is the culmination of a journey,
where the realization of a dream
and the realization of our self coincide.

0 – The Fool

Confusion

When clarity is lacking and one is overwhelmed by emotions, one must learn to create inner calm and channel one's energies constructively.

Description: A jester wearing a colorful outfit is walking towards adventure with a vulgar and preposterous attitude. A cat stares at him, while in the sky the sun and moon meet.

Key words: Abandonment of a situation to bring new strength to a project, a new place, or a new relationship; the need to act; the search for one's own identity.

Interpretation: You must leave the past behind, and take your unique vitality, idealism and fresh ideas with you. Perhaps you're going through the period of time between the germination of a project and its actual fulfillment, so you are not sure which direction to take. Whatever your choice, do not be afraid of not being understood or accepted. Even if you're going against the flow, just trust your gut feeling of what is right and you cannot go wrong.

I – The Magician

Planning

Moving freely with the mind leads to making choices and inevitably transforms dreams into projects.

Description: A young man appears busy with hammer and nail, resoling a shoe. Wears a long multi-colored coat, predominantly red – the color of energy, and a wide-brimmed hat. The scene takes place behind a hedge.

Key words: Innovative; achieving position; determination to succeed; a free and independent person.

Interpretation: You may ask yourself, "What is planning?" This card is the answer: planning is organizing your dreams according to a precise plan. This means writing them down in detail, ensuring that they respect your core values, and identifying at least three different ways to achieve them; no unachievable nor muddled goals. Remember to establish a way to recognize when you will have put them into practice – you will thus avoid wasting precious time.

II – The High Priestess

Wisdom

Inspiration comes from within us, but this does not mean to close oneself in solitude.

Description: A wise and mature looking woman stands over a chessboard, symbol of life, weighing her moves and thoughts to be formulated before acting. Her clothes are those of a priestess. In her hand she holds an open envelope in which we can glimpse a piece of written paper.

Key words: Charismatic female figure; full of possibilities; spiritual conquest.

Interpretation: Each of has our own internal set of laws to obey when we know we are right despite the prejudices of others. It may arise in moments of solitude or silence, but we can become aware of it thanks to a person of high moral stature, like the woman portrayed on the card. She can symbolize your inner self or a wise helper. When you are confused and don't know how to behave, stop to think and concentrate on yourself. This will help you understand what you should do.

III – The Empress

Formulation

Formulating a wish is a voluntary act; conscious and strong.

Description: Young, attractive, with an attentive expression painted on her face, the woman who appears in this card is portrayed sitting at a desk while listing her wishes on a sheet of paper. She is dressed in green and red, the colors of wisdom and action respectively; next to her lay a shield and a scepter.

Key words: Rational creative action; triumph of femininity; protection by a woman.

Interpretation: Finding the right words to express a desire is the beginning of manifestation. The key lies in abandoning oneself to the suggestions of the heart, which has always known all the answers.

It makes no difference what the object of your wish is: to move house or change jobs, meet a new love or take a long trip. The right words will flow spontaneously if you know how to wish with joy and conviction, without harming yourself or others.

IV – The Emperor

Inner Maturity

Independence, be it economic, spiritual or emotional, is the heart of one's identity.

Description: A loyal and serious looking man sits on a cube made of rock on the side of the road. Busy looking toward the right, the side of rationality which must prevail over instinct and the heart, he holds a compass in one hand, to better traverse the sea of life.

Key words: Ability to pacify, to command, to control, to protect; spiritual rationality; good news.

Interpretation: The figure in this card is master of his own life. He has overcome obstacles and indecision thanks to his own steadiness of character, his balance and common sense. The inner maturity invites you to put aside groundless projects and guard yourself from unreliable matches, and listen to the advice of a serious and loyal person, who has your best interest at heart and who you can trust. This person will help you take the right path.

V – The Pope

Coherence

The deepest desires are born from harmony with oneself and not from passing whims or external conditioning.

Description: A judge holds up his hand, with the task of keeping peace, ensuring justice, and building trust. He holds a mallet in his hand to knock on the table after pronouncing the sentence. Above him appears the Latin text "Dura Lex, Sed Lex" ("The law is hard, but it is the law.")

Key words: Emergence of a new ideal; open-mindedness; religious vocation.

Interpretation: Finding a teacher, a guide, a confessor who puts his or her moral rectitude and honor above any other concern, who is able to lift you from your torments and bestow on you heaven-sent help, is not always just wishful thinking. Should you be fortunate enough to meet one, remember that something sacred is about to be born. Thanks to his wisdom and diplomacy you may gain many advantages, provided you manage to maintain the maximum balance.

DURA LEX,
SED LEX

VI – The Lovers

The Law of Attraction

The ideal and the real are comparable and attract each other, but are rarely the same thing.

Description: The lips of a boy and a girl are facing each other locked into a kiss. In the background, overlooking them is a musical staff whose notes are composed of graphic symbols of Venus, the planet of love and Mars, the planet of sex.

Key words: Doing what we like to do; choice to be made; conflict; ambiguity.

Interpretation: This card wants you to reflect on your emotional state: are you optimistic? Do you work each day to get what you want? Are you able to imagine yourself already there? These are simple questions to see if you are able to focus on your goals and attract favorable circumstances to ensure success. Because your success will depend not only on having proper tools at your disposal but on your power to use them most effectively.

VII – The Chariot

Dynamism

We must act and ride the current of life with joy.

Description: A confident young man, dressed in princely robes drives a winged chariot. One wing is black and one white, a clear symbol of the dualism that governs the universe. In their unfolding they give the impression that they are heading in opposite directions, but it is a purely symbolic position that expresses willingness toward different paths.

Key words: Successful undertaking; television, film, or computer; evaluation of pros and cons.

Interpretation: Conservative thinking that has kept you from fighting to achieve your goals is beginning to recede. The wings you see on the card are those of thought, of imagination and of intellect: only when you will be more aware of your skills and your merits will you be able to take responsibility for your choices, flying far away from that which no longer satisfies you. You will then move forward to conquer your future.

VIII – Justice

Discipline

Sacrifice and perseverance light the path to achievement.

Description: Placed on a table, a precision balance weighs a heart against the feather of truth in an attempt to strike a balance between reason and sentiment.

Key words: Need to comply with social obligations; achievement certain despite taking quite some time; legal success.

Interpretation: Look at these scales: its plates are trying to find stability while they reconcile conflicting forces between them; they have a difficult task. If you find yourself in a complicated situation, remember that you have two options: you can find someone to blame, thus offloading your problems externally, or you can take the opportunity to give a more balanced aspect to your life, respecting the obligations and restrictions the new responsibilities foist upon you.

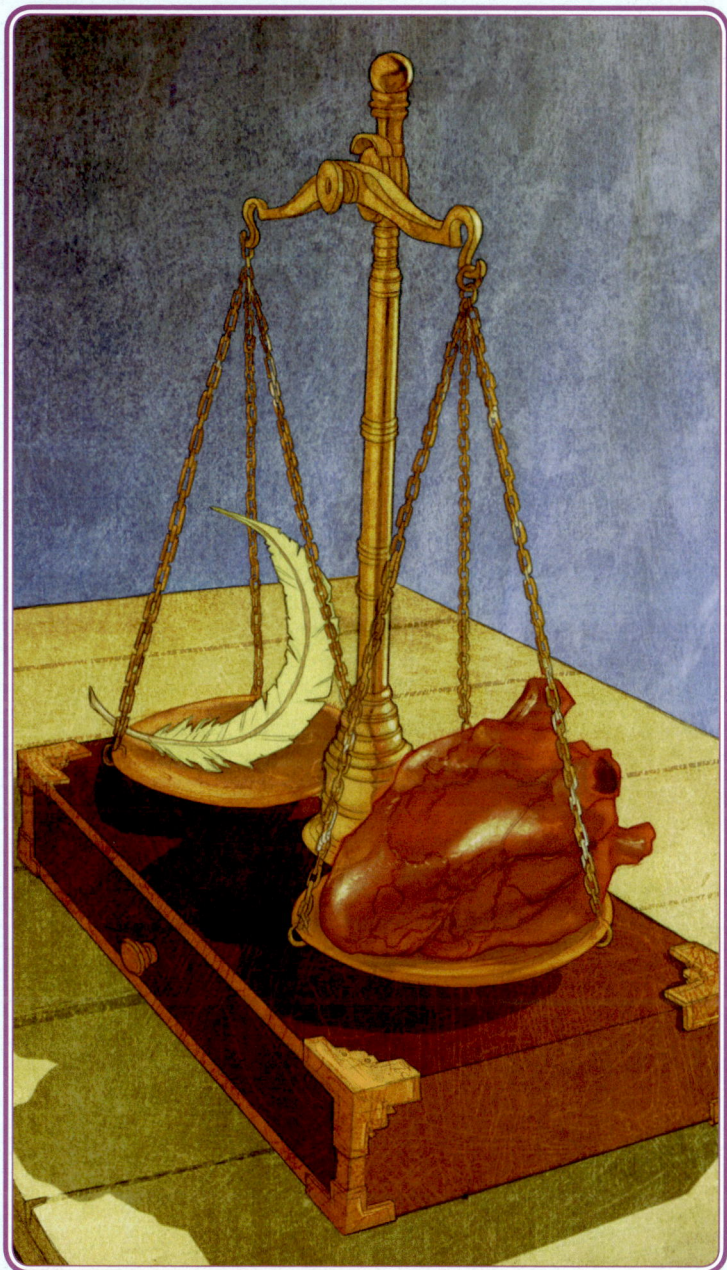

IX – The Hermit

Concentration

Patience and waiting are effective antidotes for instability and distraction.

Description: In a natural setting, an old man is meditating by observing the position of the tree: standing, the right leg bent, hands clasped over his head, eyes closed. He is wearing a dark cloak over a light garment. On the ground next to him sit a lamp and a knotted stick with a snake coiled around it. He is barefoot.

Key words: Slow but sure development; important secrets to be revealed only to those who are truly worthy; in-depth studies.

Interpretation: It happens to everyone, having a crisis or feeling alone, but you can learn to see these difficult moments in a positive light. If you seem to go too slowly or are dogged by misfortune, don't give in to depression. Seek the help of a reliable, more experienced person, capable of helping you understand that these are merely necessary obstacles to your personal development. It is the only way you can grow and acquire a clearer view of the world and its dynamics.

X – The Wheel of Fortune

The Wheel of Life

You should throw yourself into the game of life, even if everything that begins sooner or later must end.

Description: The card depicts a wheel divided into six segments: environment, health, spirit, relations, amusement, and work. Each segment in turn contains five notches, representing the degree of happiness. The environment segment is colored orange, health is yellow, the spirit is sky blue, relations is colored red, that of amusement pink and that of work is green. A finger, written with the word "input" points to the wheel.

Key words: End of a cycle; beginning of a cycle; circumstances favorable to the question.

Interpretation: You must reflect on the inevitable alternation of good times and bad times, abundance and scarcity, joy and sorrow, because life is constantly changing, encouraging progress for those who deserve it, and causing the fall of those in the wrong. If you don't wish for everything to repeat itself, with the same errors and the same dynamics, you must become aware of the mechanism that regulates this process. Put yourself at the center of the wheel and find your balance.

XI – Strength

Self Confidence

Strength is safety and stability, not violence or misuse of power. You compete against yourself, not others.

Description: Inside a forest, a beautiful, naked girl with long hair that falls onto her shoulders smothers a lion against her chest having stunned it. This shows that we must not despise the lowly but master it and use it to our advantage.

Key words: Start of an activity; combativeness; ambition.

Interpretation: You have come to a point in your life where you feel you must dare, throwing to the wind the constraints that are suffocating you. So plunge yourself head first into the beginning of something new, set free your creativity and your instincts, trust yourself. You will probably be amazed by the wave of energy that will sweep you away. Entering chaos can be scary, but if you don't, you will never become a free individual. Take courage, tomorrow you will be a new person.

XII – The Hanged Man

Doubt

Doubt is the seed of one's conscience. It must be understood and not feared.

Description: The scene depicts a young man attempting a balancing act walking on a tightrope balancing himself with his arms. The expression on his face shows preoccupation and concern, but this is the price to be paid by those who seek knowledge: nothing important and lasting can be achieved without patience and sacrifice.

Key words: A period of rest or renunciation; events adverse only in appearance; sacrifices to accept.

Interpretation: This card gives you the opportunity to dig deeper into your projects and your self-knowledge, pushing you to open yourself, to be alert, to get in touch with your inner self. Perhaps you will realize that it's not yet time to decide because the situation needs time to mature. You may need to change your perspective or see things from a different point of view. The aim is to develop your adaptability and your sense of acceptance.

XIII – Death

Change

Growth is change. Only that which changes remains faithful to itself.

Description: A beautifully colored butterfly, symbol of regeneration and metamorphosis, rests on the flowering branch of a tree, out of the cocoon in which it was enclosed, ready to spread its wings towards life with all its fascinating promises.

Key words: Beneficial renewal; beginning of a new age; radical transformation.

Interpretation: The inevitable moment has arrived to end one cycle in order to begin another. Think about what the word "transformation" means to you: what changes do you wish for? Which are already happening? Perhaps you are resisting? If so, why? Whatever your answers, keep in mind that change is necessary to evolve and progress, if you want to pass, metaphorically speaking, from the state of base metal to that of gold. It is an initial step towards rebirth and living better.

XIV –Temperance

Reflection

We must seek balance between various opposites and conflicting desires. This is not instantaneous; rather a slow process that happens gradually, day after day.

Description: A slender and graceful girl, with skin as white as milk and shiny hair cascading over her body is standing in front of a waterfall pouring over the course of a river. Nearby, a young girl goes off with a pitcher of water.

Key words: Projects carried out; hopes realized without surprises in the short term; new perspectives.

Interpretation: Our personality is based on duality: good and bad, right and wrong, positive and negative…it's too bad that this creates a conflict, often fueling strong tensions. The secret to escaping conflict and living in harmony with the dualities is to understand that we are the union of all opposites. We must consequently seek a balance, a golden mean to seal the union with our deepest nature and the environment that surrounds us.

XV – The Devil

Contrast

Some things must be confronted.

Description: Baphomet (the Devil described by the great occultist Eliphas Lévi). On his right arm, tattooed with the word SOLVE (dissolve) he holds a painting brush. On his left arm, tattoed with the word COAGULA (unify) he holds a painter 's palette, full of contrasting colors.

Key words: Advantageous contract to study carefully; obstacles overcome; need to accept destiny.

Interpretation: Perhaps up to now you have shown a face that did not belong to you, masking your deepest nature. But the prerequisite of achievement is being who you really are while recognizing and controlling your desires. This means abandoning the comforting personality, rigid and obedient, that was imposed on you, to head toward a new consciousness. If you subsequently feel that you cannot go it alone, you can ask someone for help in order to know yourself better.

XVI – The Tower

Defeat

A defeat helps check our pride and readjust our vision so we needn't start over completely.

Description: Under a stormy sky a tree is struck by lightning, breaking it. On the ground are branches and leaves. A man dressed in red, representing the strongest emotions, appears from behind while watching the scene.

Key words: Cancellation of limits; great burst of energy; healthy confrontation with reality.

Interpretation: You may have always lived in a state of unconsciousness, and now you have been hit by a sudden insight that is changing your beliefs that are guilty of being a bit too rigid. Accept, therefore, the upheaval of your life while you observe it with detachment, as if it concerned someone else. In the end, all will change for the better and you will come out stronger. Isn't it true that after the storm the air becomes invariably clearer?

XVII – The Stars

Optimism

We must find our place in the world, wait for the right moment, and build opportunities.

Description: A girl with long dark hair is sitting facing away on the calyx of a flower. She is in the lotus position. Her eyes observe a solitary bright star that shines in the sky, a sign of luck that favors the realization of the most cherished dreams.

Key words: Social contacts; artistic passion; good prospects.

Interpretation: Finally circumstances appear favorable so that you can carve out your place in the world. You feel at peace with yourself and others, because you nourish the happy sensation that fortune smiles upon you. Try to enjoy this moment without doing anything or going anywhere. Maybe this attitude of yours will make those who are used to upheaval uneasy. Remember: the insights of this period may flourish later.

XVIII – The Moon

Negative Thoughts

We mustn't fear our dark side but rather accept it without being dominated by it.

Description: A group of indistinct figures make a woman hesitate going forward on his path. In the sky is a moon represented by a silver disc with a woman's profile. Upside-down, snow-like drops float in the air as if they were attracted to the moon itself. Among the nocturnal animals present are fireflies, owls, and many bats. This scene depicts the strength and dangers of the world of appearances and imagination.

Key words: Ideal to be reached; maternal figure; darkness fading away.

Interpretation: The Moon is generally considered the lady of the subconscious par excellence, as well as the manifestation of the precious feminine quality of intuition. She invites you to go beyond the outward appearances of your wish, investigating its darker facets. Trust your instincts, they can warn you of all those impediments which, because of their faded edges can easily conceal themselves. Beware of outward appearances, errors and prejudices.

XIX – The Sun

Success

We need to confront our successes in order to grow and not stop short of realizing our dreams.

Description: This card depicts a rising sun in a cove surrounding a calm, blue sea. The daytime luminary is dispensing both heat and light. On the left is a dolphin leaping out of the water, while on the right is another about to reenter the sea.

Key words: Productive period; father figure; overcoming adversity.

Interpretation: The sun in this card radiates luck and optimism. Its rays portray a strong charge of internal energies creating intensification on a moral and psychological level. As children we are always serene, cheerful, and trusting. Then disappointment and bitterness appear and we learn that the world is not the idyllic place we thought it was. But we most recover the certainty that all will eventually be resolved for the best; the heat of the sun is always available to everyone.

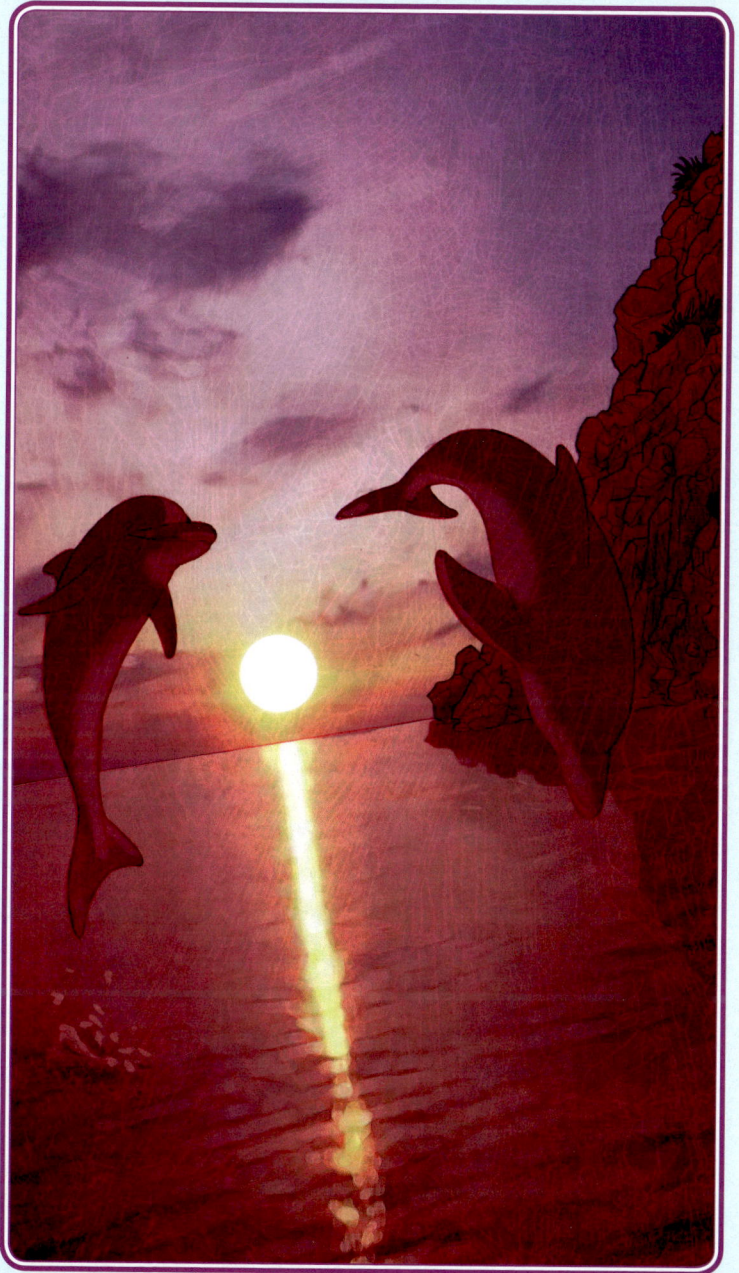

XX – Judgment

Renewal

Each end must have a corresponding beginning.

Description: Represented by the Christian iconography as an asexual creature, the essence of sweetness and spirituality, this Angel is the bearer of good news. Shown in all its power and energy, it is a true triumph of good over evil. Its large wings indicate freedom and elevation, as well as separation from the element Earth, the ability to fly and conquer the sky.

Key words: Awareness; project for the future; vocation.

Interpretation: Do not stand still in your position. It is time to change and start following your wishes. If you spend too much time thinking, you become trapped by the fear of not being able to make it. Listen to the sudden ideas that come to mind, as they might change your life. Consider them and give them a positive boost of energy by paying attention to them. Do not judge; do not stop at appearances. Try to listen with your heart, calling into question that which you previously deemed finished.

XXI – The World

Achievement

This is the culmination of a journey, where the realization of a dream and the realization of our self coincide.

Description: A puzzle shows two cherubs at the center of the card. They support a large sphere within which there is a great fantastic castle built on a rocky inlet. Behind it a rainbow lights up the sky. In the upper left corner, a hand is portrayed in the act of inserting the missing puzzle piece.

Key words: Slow but steady evolution; a stroke of luck; divine protection.

Interpretation: You have probably reached the end of an experience that has recently taken up your time and energy. This is an accomplishment, an achievement, the reaching of a goal. Do not feel sad but rather be grateful and accept the fact that life is full of many fine and new beginnings. Celebrate both: the end of the old and the beginning of the new. Do not cling to what no longer makes sense to you.

Minor Arcana

The 56 Minor Arcana are just as important as the 22 Major Arcana. They provide the detail to the answers outlined by the Major Arcana, fleshing out the delicate process that allows us to free ourselves from our negative beliefs. This is the only way to attract what we want and express our most intimate and true identity.

The Minor Arcana are numbered from one to ten; in addition there is the Knave, Knight, Queen, and King. The four suits are: Cups, Coins, Wands and Swords. Each suit symbolically represents a specific characteristics necessary to face life with this new, creative approach.

Cups

Intuitions, emotions, imagination

Cups represent intuition, emotions, and the imagination needed to visualize those life changes that up to now we believed to be impossible.

The corresponding Pythagorean symbol is Water. In astrology the following zodiac signs belong to the element of Water: Cancer, Scorpio, and Pisces.

Coins

Genuine commitment, in-depth study

Coins represent the concrete commitment and the extensive study necessary to achieve our goals, as well as the money and wealth that they can produce.

The corresponding Pythagorean element is Earth. The astrological zodiac signs belonging to the Earth element are: Taurus, Virgo, and Capricorn.

Wands
Energy, initiative, dynamism, creativity

Wands represent energy, initiative, dynamism and creativity – all indispensable energies that help our wishes come true, reminding us that laziness is never a good idea.

The corresponding Pythagorean element is Fire. The zodiac signs belonging to this element are: Aries, Leo, and Sagittarius.

Swords
Difficulties and struggles to be faced

Swords represent the difficulties and struggles that must be faced before enjoying those desires that, once achieved, will allow us to enjoy independence and personal freedom.

The corresponding Pythagorean element is Air. The astrological zodiac signs belonging to the element of Air are: Gemini, Libra, and Aquarius.

Abundance
(Ace of Cups)
Predisposition to love and be loved

Harmony
(Two of Cups)
Two elements that blend with equal intensity

The Solution
(Three of Cups)
Idealized love

Stability
(Four of Cups)
Hopes of achievement pinned on partner

Happiness
(Five of Cups)
Emotional renewal

The past
(Six of Cups)
Giving and receiving on an emotional level

Imagination
(Seven of Cups)
Amorous encounters that create hope

Opportunity
(Eight of Cups)
Deep union with divine love

Triumph
(Nine of Cups)
Justice is served

Home
(Ten of Cups)
Emotional satisfaction

The young admirer
(Knave of Cups)
Passage between childhood and adulthood

The friend
(Knight of Cups)
Youth in its overwhelming boldness

The mother
(Queen of Cups)
Charitable person inspired by faith

The professional
(King of Cups)
Enamored vision of the world

Healing
(Ace of Coins)
The concrete aspects of existence

Indecision
(Two of Coins)
Something is brewing

Leadership
(Three of Coins)
Achieved ambitions

Security
(Four of Coins)
Home and health, a territory

The Partner
(Five of Coins)
Ability to instill courage in others

Anxiety
(Six of Coins)
Small aid given or received

Progress
(Seven of Coins)
Ideas that produce income

Career
(Eight of Coins)
Wealth satisfies every need

The Conquest
(Nine of Coins)
A material stage draws to an end

Luck
(Ten of Coins)
The way of prosperity ends

The Student
(Knave of Coins)
Serious and constructive intentions

The Worker
(Knight of Coins)
Overcoming obstacles creatively

The Heiress
(Queen of Coins)
Money first

The Banker
(King of Coins)
Power based on position

The Beginning
(Ace of Wands)
A new cycle opens

Restlessness
(Two of Wands)
Motion rests on dualism

Development
(Three of Wands)
Energy aimed at a purpose

Serenity
(Four of Wands)
Events having taken shape, come to fruition

Success
(Five of Wands)
Resisting attacks of fate

Reward
(Six of Wands)
Mastery of one's own means

Negotiation
(Seven of Wands)
Union of the intellect and matter

Fulfillment
(Eight of Wands)
Forces of attraction in motion

Setback
(Nine of Wands)
Providential enlightenment

Victory
(Ten of Wands)
The cycle is complete in all its aspects

The Stranger
(Knave of Wands)
Creative project to be refined

The Bachelor
(Knight of Wands)
Channeled instincts

The Confidante
(Queen of Wands)
Foresight and telepathic skills

The Gentleman
(King of Wands)
Vital, creative, and sexual energy

Spirit of initiative
(Ace of Swords)
Victory obtained cunningly

Conflict
(Two of Swords)
Intellectual possibilities to be used

Departure
(Three of Swords)
Disorganized communication

Solitude
(Four of Swords)
Prisoner of the mind

Loss
(Five of Swords)
Cynical or hypocritical political opinions

Caution
(Six of Swords)
Watch out for reckless behavior

Hope
(Seven of Swords)
Capacity to be unselfish in order to give one's best

Crisis
(Eight of Swords)
Intellectual block

Mortification
(Nine of Swords)
Fear of losing one's individuality

Defeat
(Ten of Swords)
Possible quarrels and ingratitude

The Guardian
(Knave of Swords)
Prudence and perseverance

The Fighter
(Knight of Swords)
Solution of a problem

The Rival
(Queen of Swords)
Vindictive intelligence

The Professor
(King of Swords)
Obeying the rules and laws

Ace of Cups

Abundance

Predisposition to love and be loved.

Description: The card has a cornucopia overflowing with fruits. This is an image that appears often in allegorical paintings, illustrations in books, or in mythological trappings of old tapestries. It symbolizes fertility and promise for the future, as well as illusions and reliance on luck.

Keywords: Emotional satisfaction, the birth of a love or a child, emotional family ties.

Interpretation: Assigning a value to the differences of character of the other person is the best attitude in order to overcome inevitable conflicts, but also to open oneself to the pleasant surprises that a relationship can offer. Learn to consider the people involved in a relationship as if they were two complementary colors such as yellow and blue: when viewed individually, they are two separate and different colors; if, however, they can get along, they blend together and create a new color, green.

Two of Cups

Harmony

Two elements that blend with equal intensity

Description: Yin and Yang, a symbol that permeates the whole of Chinese philosophy as two opposing primary energies, in this case represents Day and Night on a blue background. The black portion Yin depicts a starry sky where a full moon shines, while the white Yang shows a clear sky from which rays of light filter.

Keywords: Artistic affinity; new depth in an existing relationship or the beginning of a new one; thirst for love.

Interpretation: The soul mate, that perfect partner that "somewhere must exist," that holder of all virtues and incapable of disappointing, in reality does not exist. Whether or not you are in a stable relationship, you must keep this in mind, because the need to find your true love might make you miss more than one opportunity while real life passes you by. Often you find happiness right next to someone we "never would have thought…"

Three of Cups

The Solution

Idealized love

Description: The key that appears in this image, inserted into a lock, is the quintessential instrument of enterprise, of change, and of accomplishment; the time has come to take an important decision. There are many keys, for different locks.

Keywords: Ardent rediscovery of love; romanticism; romantic plans.

Interpretation: Being in love is not enough to feed desire, because passion nourishes itself on mystery and surprise. Betrayal, real or perceived, for example, is a great driving force of desire. But that which really rekindles attraction is the fear of loss, and this fear manifests itself only if the other person is free and shows his or her own individuality. Therefore, if you long to reawaken your eroticism, don't forget that jealousy, the fear of losing one's partner, and uncertainty can all be powerful aphrodisiacs.

Four of Cups

Stability

Hopes of achievement pinned on partner

Description: The column is an architectural element that holds great importance in all the religions of the past: in Israel the columns of Solomon's Temple represented cosmic balance. In Egypt, its function as a support prevailed: the Zed pillar is the backbone of Osiris, the symbol of life itself. For the Greeks, the column was a phallic symbol and as an attribute of Demeter, symbolized fertility.

Keywords: Search for emotional security or family harmony; overly materialistic love; self-doubt.

Interpretation: Whether it is with your friends, your partner, or your children, perhaps when you talk about your affections you focus too much on quantity as opposed to quality. You need to learn that the expressions "give a lot" or "receive little" only roughly define the feelings you feel. In relationships that grow, both your expectations and those of the other person must escape the logic of quantity. Seek, rather, to assess the quality of care and understanding that you give and receive.

Five of Cups

Happiness

Emotional renewal

Description: A field of sunflowers enjoys the warm rays of the sun on a beautiful summer's day. Regarding this flower, mythology has it that Clytia – who out of jealousy had her sister sentenced to death, transformed by Apollo into a plant – underwent her own metamorphosis: she became a sunflower, always forced to turn her head towards the sun god she was madly in love with and who had abandoned her for her rival.

Keywords: Return of a loved one; favorable development of an emotional issue; possible difficulties due to one's own contradictions.

Interpretation: As in the tantric philosophy, the quest for orgasm is not the first prerequisite of sexual intercourse. Balance in a couple is achieved by harmony between the partners that goes beyond sensual pleasure. There is a need for a deep and intimate exchange in which the union includes not only the body, but the spirit as well. Candles, incense, or scented oils may help create an atmosphere of intimacy and togetherness.

Six of Cups

The Past

Giving and receiving on an emotional level

Description: A large hour-glass, symbol of time and of Saturn, the god that governs it, reminds us that the sand or water inside it could be a secret knowledge reserved to initiates, or otherwise a source of wisdom offered to disciples who go looking for it. Beside it, a man is depicted in the act of moving away, keeping one hand in his pocket.

Keywords: Return of the past and the reawakening of feelings never buried; general love that includes the intellect, the heart and instinct; excessive self-indulgence.

Interpretation: Perhaps you have always considered romantic love as a key ingredient of marriage. This is not quite accurate, as marriage is actually a contract, and has been as such for centuries, long before love became the main component. It can last if it turns into a successful partnership based on shared values and mutual respect. If you are getting married or are having difficulties with your spouse, remember that a good marriage allows love to blossom, not the other way around.

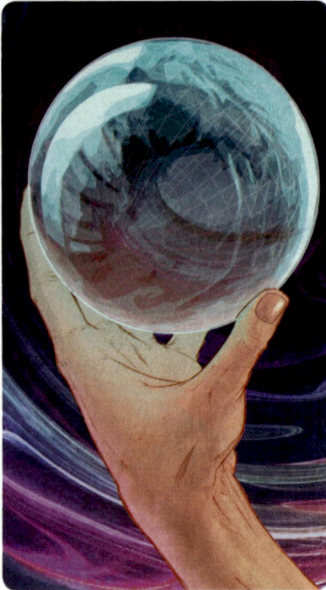

Seven of Cups

Imagination

Amorous encounters that create hope

Description: A multi-colored crystal ball, a true catalyst of energy capable of capturing the vibrations of the astral plane, appears resting on the palm of a hand. Its reflections radiate not only on the hand but on the surrounding environment as well.

Keywords: Dreams and illusions; positive conclusion of a relationship; the power of goodness; the power of conscious love.

Interpretation: You're probably a hedonist without complexes, and thus you refuse the appeals of society, only pretending to conform and only if you feel like it. You can feel free to say yes or no, because to you sexuality is not a means to reassure yourself of your seductive powers. Attentive as you are to the happiness of the body, why not go further? Perhaps you could try exoticism. Different cultures can suggest an infinite number of practices to experience.

Eight of Cups

Opportunity

Deep union with divine love

Description: A pair of red dice turn on a light blue background, showing from one to six points etched on their sides. The image invites the tempting of fate, or entrusting one's fate to chance.

Keywords: End of a relationship and the beginning of another, better than the first; profitable business; perseverance in affections.

Interpretation: Your heart is open and full of love; it drives you to love life and its joys. Consequently, your presence makes others happy, and you know how to bring out the best in them. If you are not currently in harmony with yourself, your partner, or those around you, let go of the propensity to judge and relax. Only if you know how to ride through your pain and understand it will your happiness be reborn.

Nine of Cups

Triumph

Justice is served

Description: Two pairs of hands lift a trophy in the air, which stands glittering against the sky. Perhaps you are about to claim victory because you have overcome or are about to overcome your difficulties. Beware, however, of narcissism that might make you feel more successful than you really are.

Keywords: Recognizing one's own merits; happiness in love; need to get away from something that no longer has a reason to exist.

Interpretation: If you want to free yourself of something or someone who is making you suffer, face your demons and your weaknesses, as there is no change without self-knowledge. Look at your past and why you always repeat the same mistakes. Explain why you are ill at ease: this may help both you and your partner to understand your mistakes, and to maybe re-establish the groundwork for a relationship or setting up a more authentic life.

Ten of Cups

Home

Emotional satisfaction

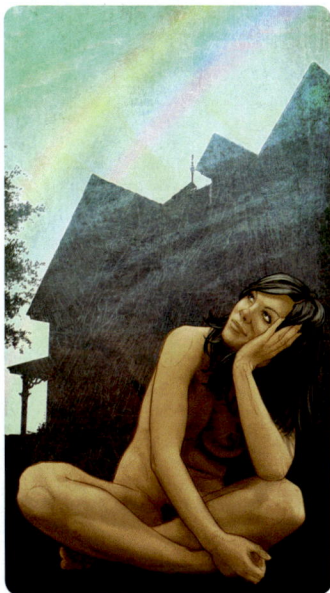

Description: A naked girl is sitting cross-legged in the outline of a house, calling to mind the purest sense of beauty as nature created it in its profound wisdom. In this case the house is a projection of our personality, of how we are or how we would like to be.

Keywords: City, birthplace, residence; sentimental achievement; happiness and harmony.

Interpretation: You possess a sweetness that heals wounds, ensuring your partner or others feel loved for who they are, without needing to change or give up being themselves. If at this time you are unable to free yourself from your fears or if you are projecting them on those around you, let go of aggression and choose the way of kindness, which is the cornerstone of your balance. Find aspects to love unconditionally, in yourself and in others, and your fears will vanish.

Knave of Cups

The young admirer

Passage from childhood to adulthood

Description: A young man is intent on ringing the doorbell of a house. One hand is hidden behind his back and holds a bouquet of red roses, the symbol of ardent passion. These flowers are connected to Venus and feeling of love. Legend has it that roses were originally only white, and that red roses came to be when a few drops of Venus's blood, scratched by their thorns while rescuing her wounded lover, fell on their petals.

Keywords: Loving friendship; fear and desire for love; a friend or a trusted and affectionate collaborator.

Interpretation: Perhaps your most intimate desires scare you a bit, given that the idea of abandoning self-control is blocking you and feeding your stress. Most likely your upbringing, the relationship you have with your body, and your natural shyness represent obstacles. In fact you have a remarkable and as yet unexplored erotic potential, all you have to do is develop it. To do so, relax the mind and body by practicing yoga, dance, or biofeedback.

Suit of Cups

Knight of Cups

The friend

Youth in its overwhelming boldness

Description: The card depicts a handshake, which refers to friendship and confidence. The hand is a symbol that embodies human activity and the concept of possession or ownership. It represents a link between the physical energies of man and those of heaven, and can also become a therapeutic tool charged with magnetic force, or the executor of the magic gesture that creates and revokes.

Keywords: Humanitarian undertaking; sincere love; infidelity or licentiousness

Interpretation: It may be that you are a prisoner of multiple identities. Throughout your day, you play the role of parent, employee, spouse or partner, friend, and so on. To rediscover your inner source of wisdom you should take a moment each day to gather yourself and meditate. This will help you blend and harmonize all the aspects of your life, allowing you to discover the real you.

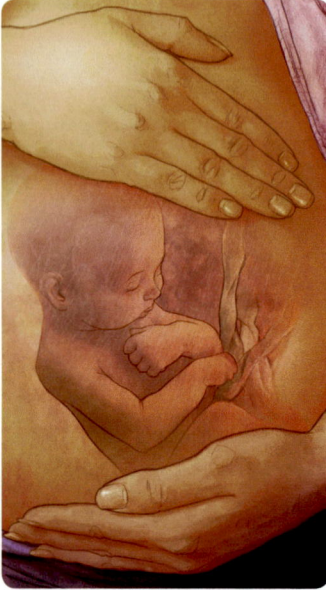

Queen of Cups

The mother

Charitable person inspired by faith

Description: The image of a pregnant belly, inside of which appears, in detail, a fetus, can be taken as an evolution and maturation, but also as a renewal. The time in the womb alludes on a symbolic level to a period of stagnation, designed to nurture and to transform the unconscious forces. This image may also refer to an idea that is in gestation, waiting to sweetly come to light.

Keywords: Beloved woman, be it a lover, companion, or mother; pure femininity; selfless love.

Interpretation: Often it is thanks to a great disappointment that you can learn to truly love. The expectations your parents taught you fade away. Once you find yourself alone you can confront your suffering, learning to see more clearly what is really important inside yourself. You must simply free yourself of illusions, allowing the unconscious to choose for you.

King of Cups

The professional

Enamored vision of the world

Description: A business-man in a meeting uses a pointer to show a chart on the wall. Capable of grand actions based on his enam-ored vision of the world, he is an honest person who you can definitely trust.

Keywords: Man full of love or one who seeks a com-panion; joy of living; faith-fulness and harmony in the couple.

Interpretation: When it comes to start a relationship, physi-cal attraction is key and non-negotiable. Indeed this is what will give you an edge over the "storms" that a couple faces. It is not a question of aesthetic perfection, but rather smells, gestures, tone of voice, sensations. This is why you mustn't compromise. Who courts you may be an excellent friend, but will become your partner only if you really like his or her body and character.

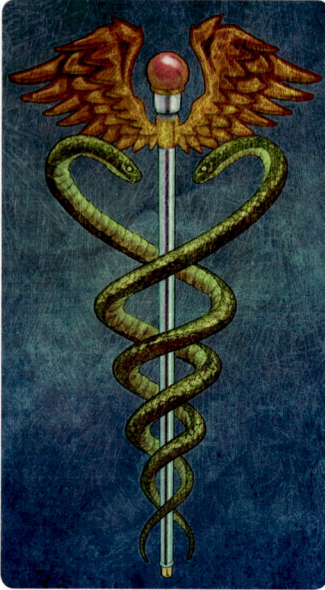

Ace of Coins

Healing

The concrete aspects of existence

Description: The staff of Asclepius, Greek god of medicine and healing, is represented by a stick around which two serpents are intertwined, a symbol of intuition that springs from first hand knowledge of nature. At the top of the staff are two small wings and a globe.

Keywords: The power of money and material goods; family life, health, home; contract.

Interpretation: You're convinced that money is a tool that allows you psychological wellbeing and the ability to develop and grow. Millionaires, in your opinion, not only have money, but above all, the attitude and mentality of those who know they create their own destiny. To be rich, in short, is a lifestyle that can offer more opportunities, more freedom, and more choices. To become rich, you believe, is not a privilege reserved for the few, but a question of having the right approach to life.

Two of Coins

Indecision

Something is brewing

Description: A young woman finds herself at a crossroads and is clearly undecided about which way to go: perhaps to the right, giving precedence to common sense and inner discipline or to the left, giving free rein to the bizarre, the fascinating and mystery that lies within her.

Keywords: Financial project in gestation or house under construction; material interests; diverse and contradicting aspects to be examined in respect to a question.

Interpretation: To have a big house, to enjoy holidays in exotic places, or to achieve economic independence are only the results of a dream. Many people cling to what they achieved long ago, but some are afraid to dream because they fear failure, and therefore won't take responsibility for successes as well as failures. Donald Trump was right when he said, "Plan your future to become a billionaire, whatever happens you'll at least be a millionaire!"

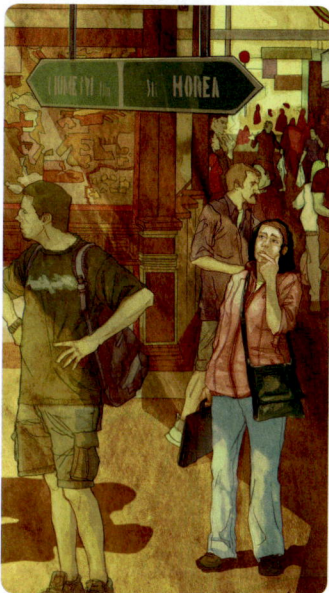

Three of Coins

Leadership

Achieved ambitions

Description: An orchestral conductor is busy conducting, while standing on a red platform. His figure reminds us that we all have the need for a guide at particular times of our lives. He is also the personification of the superego, which controls our drives and points us in the best direction.

Keywords: Material investment with an uncertain outcome; financial risk; travel expenses and study fees.

Interpretation: Many people don't have the ability to earn, maintain, and manage a large sum of money. But since in life you always have to deal with money, it is important to understand how it works. Each of the three stages mentioned above implies new strategies, new knowledge, and new skills, and each of these is more influenced by psychological than technical know-how. Therefore, if you want to obtain different financial results, you must first change your attitude.

Four of Coins

Safety

Home and health, a territory

Description: The word PASSWORD appears in bold letters on a computer screen, followed by a white space in which to type. With it you can enter the borderless world that is the Internet, or check your e-mail. Furthermore, the use of a password was already fashionable in ancient times, especially in the military. Guards would demand it of anyone who approached, allowing only those who knew it to pass.

Keywords: Fortune and financial stability; death and rebirth; sales and acquisitions.

Interpretation: If you are looking for concrete results in the financial realm, you need to know that they depend on your actions, which in turn depend on your state of mind. Only the ability to put yourself in right state of mind allows you to successfully perform targeted actions. If you want to earn more, you must eliminate everything from your psychological approach to money that blocks you or scares you, such as fear, anxiety, or negative moods.

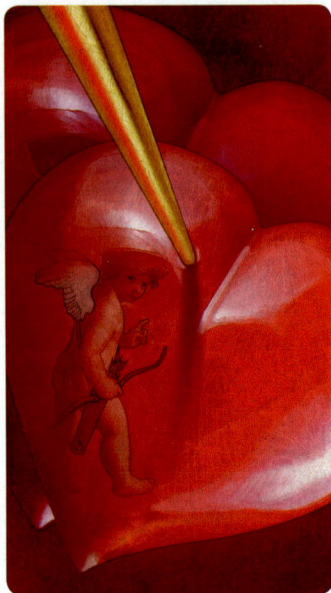

Five of Coins

The partner

Ability to instill courage in others

Description: Two red hearts, one above the other, both show the same golden arrow passing through them, from side to side. The heart represents the center of man, his inner sun, the fire of his feelings and his passions. From the cruelly snatched heart of Zagreus, Dionysus is reborn: it thus contains the symbol of life itself, the seed of rebirth, while the arrow, which is that of Cupid, is a symbol of passionate and meteoric love.

Keywords: Strong sexual attraction; investments in clean energy and in alternative therapies; evolution of a financial situation.

Interpretation: One of the most common limiting beliefs is that "it takes money to make money." What happens if you begin to believe such a thing, that until you have money you won't be able to earn more? If those around you are not good role models for changing the way you relate to money, then expand your circle of acquaintances. Read, study, and attend courses. Only then will the barriers that hinder you begin to fall.

Six of Coins

Anxiety

Small aid given or received

Description: The cigarette satisfies an oral pleasure that goes back to the time of suckling our mother's milk. Having the desire to smoke refers to a subtle pleasure in our past. On this card the cigarette is portrayed in an upright position, and sitting on top is a young man visibly worried.

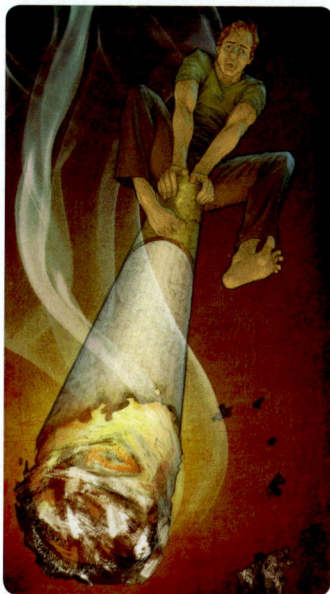

Keywords: Enjoyment of well managed money; sense of beauty; gastronomy, sensuality.

Interpretation: If your reason for improving your financial conditions comes from negative emotions such as fear, anger, or the need to prove something to yourself, then money will fail to make you happy. Instead, try spending it to take your parents to some place they could never afford or to help someone in difficulty. In this case not only will those who benefited will be filled with joy but so will your mind and your thoughts.

Seven of Coins

Progress

Ideas that produce income

Description: Five chairs lined up inside a room depict the gradual but continuous evolution that occurred in their design: you begin with a simple stool to arrive at an ergonomic chair. Generally chairs are connected to life, which can be wealthy if the chair is comfortable, or difficult if the chair is unstable.

Keywords: Money spent to advance humanity; global success of an enterprise; all that is undertaken is likely to grow.

Interpretation: Once you have found the right way and the correct mindset, earning more money is like driving a car. In the beginning it seems difficult – you have to pay attention to the clutch, the rearview mirror, the gearbox, and so many other things – but then after a while it becomes second nature; you get in the car, turn on the engine and go. Just remember that if you don't believe that your path towards prosperity is a question of practice, then somehow you will try to sabotage it, even subconsciously.

Suit of Coins

Eight of Coins

Career

Wealth satisfies every need

Description: A young businesswoman with her arms crossed over her chest and a determined expression is waiting for something or someone. She is wearing a suit and high heels, and at her feet is a briefcase. She is in an urban environment, hinting at socializing, self-realization through work, and interesting relationships.

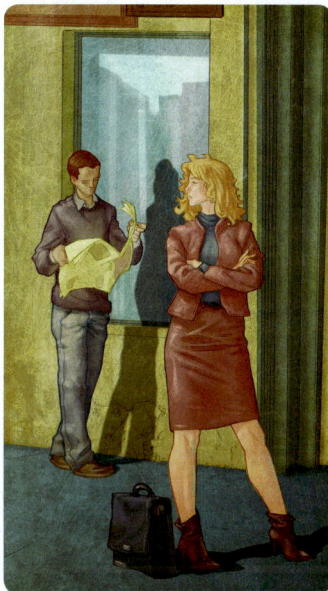

Keywords: Harmony and prosperity; craftsmanship; a meeting that brings earnings.

Interpretation: Your mind has the ability to focus on the positive or on the negative, on problems or on their solutions. If you acquire the ability to create empowering questions for yourself, you will be able to change your mood and always be able to find a solution. Try asking yourself: how can I create additional revenue? How can I organize my life so that money is no longer a problem? If you do it frequently, your brain will begin to provide better answers more quickly.

Nine of Coins

The conquest

A material stage draws to an end

Description: A ladder appears resting on the symbol for the euro, which may represent financial worries, greed, the desire for wealth but also the need for affection or the desire to measure one's own value. At the top stands a little man with a triumphant air.

Keywords: Financial change that results in a new project; material detachment; ability to positively guide others.

Interpretation: Before you achieve anything you must dream of it or imagine it. Being able to manage the positive images of what you would like to do offers you the unique opportunity to become the master of your destiny, even if the image alone is not sufficient. Above all you must act, because action is what transforms your dreams into results. Furthermore, if it is true that not everyone who dreams get results, it is equally true that all those who get results are dreamers.

Ten of Coins

Luck

The way of prosperity completes

Description: Amongst some fortune cookies there is one that is broken. From inside it spouts a note with a message to be interpreted, but it appears incomprehensible given that you can see some letters but you can't grasp the words or their meanings. Thus is the rest of our life, with clear pages alternating with confused, fragmented ones.

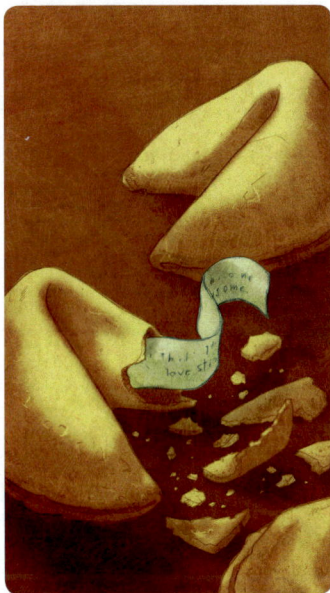

Keywords: Wealth and prosperity; good fortune that arrives after a lifetime of work; inheritance.

Interpretation: Words can change experiences you have had and can have. Analyze your language when you talk about money and identify the emotion it provokes in you. Is it negative, causing you look at and touch money with disdain and mistrust, or does it spur you to improve your financial circumstances, making you do your best to increase your income? Whatever it is, don't forget that money is energy: the more you have, the more you can build up.

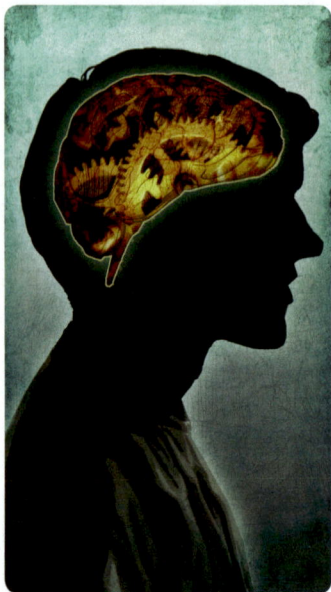

Knave of Coins

The student

Serious and constructive intentions

Description: In the profile of a human head, in the part that houses the brain a series of gears are highlighted: these point to the tireless mental work necessary in life. In Plato's dialogue, Timaeus, he says that the human head is "imago mundi": each head is a world unto itself, the very life of its owner, the best of his or her being.

Keywords: Indecision in face of a physical or financial danger; excessive self-confidence; the ability to give the right value to money.

Interpretation: Words are never uttered at random and metaphors describe what is happening in your mind and in the minds of others. Once you understand the emotional state expressed by the metaphor, it becomes easier to change it, and perhaps choose a more positive one. Ask yourself: what is the metaphor you use to describe your financial situation? What does money mean to you? How do you judge the wealthy? And above all, which metaphor can you create to have money in abundance?

Knight of Coins

The worker

Overcoming obstacles creatively

Description: This card portrays a man's profile busy working on a computer. He's wearing a white shirt with the sleeves rolled up, a sports watch, and intellectual-looking glasses. The interpretation reflects the Hindu concept of Karma: each person's particular task assigned in this life is a consequence to that person's conduct in a previous life and the caste to which he or she belongs. According to this system of thought, justness consists of performing one's own duties, and not those of others, with resignation and serenity.

Keywords: Travel; quest for one's place in the universe; money invested to create something new.

Interpretation: Becoming rich means making decisions, particularly financial ones, each day. This is why it is important to put yourself in a physical state of total and absolute stability. When you are standing, keep your head up high, and try to feel your feet firmly on the ground as if they had roots. Your breathing should be calm and sure, and your body's center of gravity low. This position, borrowed from martial arts, will allow you to see problems differently.

Queen of Coins

The heiress

Money first

Description: A middle aged blonde, wearing the latest fashion and with a puppy under her arm, is walking down the hallway of a luxury hotel with a casual air. Her appearance reveals that her money and her position are important to her, which leads her to have contrasting attitudes: at times she deploys a considerable amount of energy to maintain things as they are, other times she knows how to renew things with unexpected projects. She is followed by a porter carrying her bags.

Keywords: Greed for money and power, but also generosity; ability to preserve one's assets; feelings sacrificed for the sake of power.

Interpretation: The most limiting state of mind you will have to face on the road to financial wellbeing is fear. Fear is merely a mental state that is generated by five factors: beliefs, focus, images, internal dialogue, and body language. Those who fear use their bodies in a specific way, believe in determined things, have a certain internal dialogue and visualize images that portray the motives of their fear. But the courageous person isn't the one who isn't afraid, but the one who, despite this, takes action.

King of Coins

The banker

Power based on position

Description: A man with an air of maturity, richly experienced, is sitting at his desk. He is impeccably dressed. Behind him is an open safe with a large amount of money inside. He could be a very wealthy man or one completely indifferent to money living in the miraculous prosperity of the present.

Keywords: Valuable experience in regards to money and real estate; charity; savvy investments.

Interpretation: According to experts, getting rich is 95% psychology and 5% technique, because it's not what you know that makes the difference, but what you do with that knowledge. To make use of the information you have, you must enter the frame of mind that allows you to use it and act to achieve new results. Observe, therefore, how your moods come about, how they can be changed, and how you can use them to gain true freedom, which includes financial freedom as well.

Ace of Wands

The beginning

A new cycle begins

Description: An evocative dawn illuminates a cheerful, enjoyable, and richly colored landscape, with a clear sky and fine air. The view instills a sense of renewal and thus the desire to move forward towards new goals.

Keywords: Desire and sexual potency; creativity in an unusual context; courage in difficulties.

Interpretation: Stand in front of a mirror and ask yourself, "How can I channel the enormous amount of energy I have? In my work? In my personal relationships? In my relationship with my children?" Think back to situations where you did not use it properly, then answer these questions out loud. Pay attention to the signals that your body and your voice send you. These clues will help you identify your mood and your confidence level, and will be able to make the best choice.

Two of Wands

Restlessness

Motion rests on dualism

Description: The shadow of a deformed being is projected on the walls and is being observed by a perplexed but respectable looking man. This is the other side of his personality, that which he refuses to acknowledge because it represents the "negative part of oneself." For him, it is the one in which instinct governs over reason.

Keywords: Radical change; the need to put an end to a hesitation; contrasts; antagonism.

Interpretation: On the road to awareness you will have many doubts. They will test your desire to change. By questioning your desire for change, you will strengthen and legitimize it. This mustn't frighten you, as change means taking risks, exploring unknown territories, and living in uncertainty for a period of time. When your discomfort becomes unbearable and the benefits you stand to gain from change outweigh the possible disadvantages, you will know for certain that it is time.

Three of Wands

Development

Energy aimed at a purpose

Description: This card portrays a farmer busy sowing. A strange light warms up the sky, accentuating how everything in life comes to an end that lead to new beginnings, including hope, illusions, romantic relationships, and friendships.

Keywords: Business or work communications; explosion of vital energy; creative impulses.

Interpretation: When you take a shortcut or postpone decisions, you block the development of your potential. The time has come to take the initiative to make changes in your life. Look toward the future if you want to analyze the present with clarity. Forget the past and regrets of missed opportunities. This forward focus will give you the courage to make uncomfortable choices to create the life you want and leave all regrets behind.

Four of Wands

Serenity

*Events, having taken shape,
come to fruition*

Description: In a green
meadow, the grass swaying
in the wind, sits a girl in a
white organza dress with a
blade of grass between her
teeth. Her feet are bare,
bringing to mind self confidence and confidence in
action. She also wears a
wide-brimmed straw hat to
protect her from the intem-
perance of the sun.

Keywords: Solid and fruitful friendships; crowning of an enterprise; associations for a common goal.

Interpretation: Think about the meaning of the word "trans-
gress." In the etymological sense of the word it means "advance"
or "push oneself forward." It is what you need right now when
everything seems to be going well. Try to continuously focus
outside of yourself, towards your desired future. Consider it
the only way to be yourself. Try experimenting and living in
a world of constant surprise, exploring the unknown dimen-
sions of yourself and the world. You will discover a natural
desire that is part of your existence and your being.

Five of Wands

Success

Resisting attacks of fate

Description: A windmill - a symbol of love of work, wealth, and prosperity - is shown with the blades in motion while the summer sun's rays caress its contours making it shine in the midst of the countryside.

Keywords: Conflict between sexuality and spirituality; evolution toward unexpected depths; resistance to the attacks of fate.

Interpretation: According to experts, you do not become the lead actor of your own life all of a sudden. If you wish to free yourself from habits, start by changing the most banal gestures. Acting with renewed vitality on a daily basis is the best way to profoundly transform yourself. Rejoice in every small step forward, without being too demanding or in a hurry to change. Grant yourself the necessary time for your metamorphosis. Don't forget to be mindful of others who must adjust to you evolution.

Six of Wands

Reward

Mastery of one's own means

Description: In the midst of a summer's day, full of light and heat, a man in a wheat field seems intent on harvesting the weat, a true promise of wishes fulfilled.

Keywords: Accomplishment of unexpected things; continuous activity; full days.

Interpretation: It is not the time to withdraw into yourself but rather a time of action. Pick a specific wish to make a reality and act immediately. There are likely numerous possibilities, so focus on the one you think is most effective. Remember that the future already exists because it is the long-term effects of your action. You must assume the risk of living, learning to tolerate uncertainty and the fears that will inevitably accompany you.

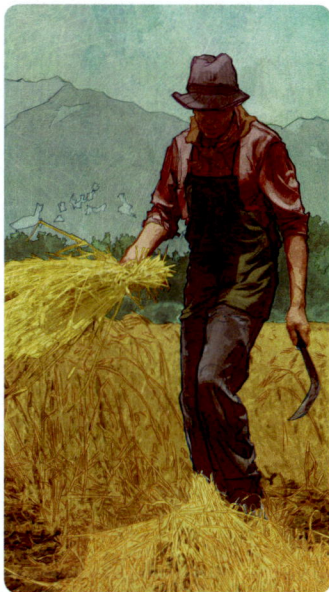

Seven of Wands

Negotiation

Union of intellect and matter

Description: Seated before a frame, a woman is busy weaving fabric, weaving the weft with a shuttle through the warp threads. Her image evokes the incessant and focused constructive activity of those who wish to realize their dreams.

Keywords: Success and benefits in all fields; creativity; solidarity.

Interpretation: Congratulations, you now have what you wanted. But that does not mean that you have to stop setting yourself new goals. Try to realize a dream you previously put aside in order to focus on other dreams. Be curious, accept new risks, learn something new whenever you can. The important thing is not to rest on your laurels but to achieve genuine harmony between intention and action. Then the victory you just acquired can become a key to open the hidden door of a new talent.

Eight of Wands

Fulfillment

Forces of attraction in motion

Description: A bowl full of whipped cream sits in all its splendor on a table, recalling in popular terms the concepts of luck, wealth, and personal success. Next to it lies the whisk used to whip the cream.

Keywords: A project to be carried out with consent of the family or associates; high hopes for the future; transformation.

Interpretation: The card suggests you devote all your energy to realizing your dream, making a timely and effective decision. A fundamental rule for success is to follow your instinct. Too often we do not listen to our body's reaction, which is too bad because we can access much inherent wisdom there. If your heart beats too loudly or your stomach turns, these are clear indications that the road in front of you is not for you.

Nine of Wands

Setback

Providential enlightenment

Description: A foot wearing a summer shoe steps accidentally into a puddle, whose murky water is a metaphor for stepping outside of one's ethical boundaries. The mud can be seen as a projection of the part of us created from, perhaps, an overly moralistic upbringing.

Keywords: Openness to knowledge; studies, exams, competitions; the need to be patient and think.

Interpretation: If you encounter obstacles, don't get discouraged. Instead, resort to your imagination and explore new ways to put your plans into practice. The secret to not losing your enthusiasm is simple. Imagine being a pianist who has played the same piece thousands of times but at each performance is able to infuse new life to the same melody, changing the tones slightly or introducing a small detail to give freshness to each note.

Ten of Wands

Victory

The cycle is complete in all its aspects

Description: A cargo ship enters port in triumph, greeted by a happy group of people who have apparently waited quite some time for its arrival. The ship represents travel and the desire to go far beyond the limits of life itself, while the port symbolizes reaching a goal after a long period of searching.

Keywords: Spiritual realization; migration abroad; positive transformations in all areas.

Interpretation: Have you reached a consistent level of satisfaction in all areas of your life, including relationships, career, home, and family? If not, maybe you need to learn that small daily efforts can lead to big satisfaction. And that's not all: the first step to take is to understand in which sector you feel the least fulfilled and commit yourself to improve it.

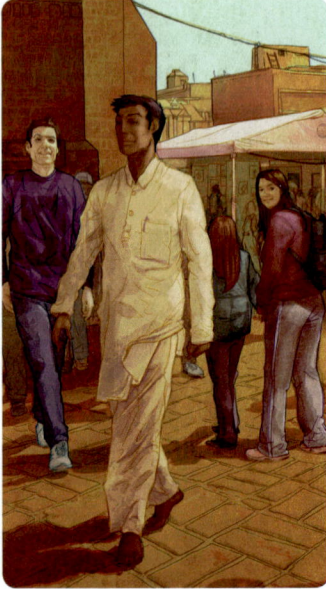

Knave of Wands

The stranger

Creative project to be refined

Description: A youth dressed like a pilgrim walks along the road with the air of one who has traveled far. He wears a distracted expression, as if the concerns for duty and responsibilities incumbent on each of us do not affect him. Passersby look at him with curiosity.

Keywords: Doubt between doing and not doing, creating and not creating, obeying or not our own wishes; energy to be channeled; good news.

Interpretation: Perhaps the time has come to stop making the best of a bad job. If it is bad, it should end so you can do something that really agrees with you. So find your desire, indulge it, and cultivate it with determination, without worrying about the aspirations of others. Don't trade your life for a cage that for all its outward beauty is still a cage. There are no mandatory choices, only redirected desires.

Knight of Wands

The bachelor

Channeled instincts

Description: A dark-haired man is leaning on the counter at a bar. He is dressed casually and observes the coming and goings inside the locale with the air of someone who wants to conquer and contemplate, but without being subjected to the influence of others.

Keywords: Proposal for change of residence; quick decision for a transformation; voluntary abandonment of the pleasures of the world.

Interpretation: The need to possess objects, especially if they are not essential such as a second cell phone, a third TV, or the latest navigation system, is making you take time and resources away from more important needs, such as family and health. Recover your internal energies by listening to your desires. Remember that self-realization is a journey through two paths. The internal subjective path requires time to identify the dreams of your soul. The external objective path asks you to reconsider your work and how you express the dreams of your soul in the world.

Queen of Wands

The confidante

Foresight and telepathic skills

Description: A charming, fair-haired woman is wearing a plaid blazer with a classic feminine cut, over a light-colored blouse. She appears to be a loyal friend as well as a good counselor.

Keywords: Valuable guidance in both the intellectual as well as moral sense; independence; opportunity to live off one's own creativity.

Interpretation: Take a few minutes each day for a month to draw up a list: on one side put down your abilities and qualities, on the other the weak points you resolve to improve upon. Be sincere and don't judge what you write down. After 30 days, review your list. Reread what you wrote and you will discern some contradictions, because you have many complex facets. Only by looking at them as a whole will you learn to recognize and emphasize your positive sides as well as your limits.

King of Wands

The gentleman

Creative, sexual, and vital energy

Description: A middle aged man with a noble expression sits comfortably in an armchair in an elegant living room, with one leg slightly crossed over the other. He exudes an aura of old-style respectability.

Keywords: Capable and respected person in professional circles; loyalty; joyful events.

Interpretation: You probably already possess the requirements for having satisfying relationships and making others feel at ease. Sometimes, however, your need to make a good impression, to find confirmation, and to be loved can override your most authentic emotional needs, thus ensnaring you in superficial relationships. Be sure to connect your social skills and the desire to please others with who you really are. Behave consistently even if by doing so you risk the disapproval of others.

Ace of Swords

Spirit of initiative

Victory obtained through cunning

Description: A snowboarder executes a jump on his board on a snowy slope. This figure symbolizes elevation, initiative, and dynamism, as well as the waiting, the absolute concentration on one's own actions. It can also represent a reversal of perspective and a reminder of the saying, "if you want to see straight, stand on your head."

Keywords: Cunning, intelligence, determination; ability to take a position; verbal aggression.

Interpretation: Being the hero of your life doesn't necessarily mean having a grandiose destiny or achieving extraordinary goals. Instead it is a feeling of being alive, experiencing the pleasure of everything in your life being in harmony with who you are. It is a space where your talents shine and where you remain flexible enough to react to new circumstances with grace and effectiveness. Learn to unfold your wings starting at the deepest center of yourself. Then you will be able to express your uniqueness and appreciate that of others.

Two of Swords

Conflict

Intellectual possibilities to be used

Description: The arms of two different people, dressed in different colored jackets, face each other with closed fists. The fist indicates an introverted attitude and the inability to communicate, just as the open hand is an indication of openness towards others, of generosity, and of extroversion.

Keywords: Equal forces in the field creating respect and esteem; enemies abandon their plans; risk of identifying oneself with certain clichés.

Interpretation: Often when you get close to your wish you stop and seek the opinion of others. This is a dangerous practice because the advice you receive will highlight contradictions instead of clarifying your thoughts. As a result, you will delay taking further action. As you procrastinate and contemplate other people's idea, time passes and you begin to miss opportunities. Then doubts and frustration can completely wipe out your self-esteem. This is why you should stop dragging your feet.

Three of Swords

Departure

Disorganized communication

Description: A plane sails through the sky, indicating a strong desire to move forward and to change our setting. The plane is in fact the desire to escape everyday life, symbol of flight and breaking loose from 'terra firma,' soaring to new heights. Inside this metaphor of take-off (the excitement), the flight (orgasm) and landing (relaxation), lies all the power of sexuality that we hide in our deepest part.

Keywords: Desire for intellectual development; doubt, diffidence; difficult collaboration, individualism.

Interpretation: Often the world of work require you to work in groups, but this isn't always easy. You often need to create a collaborative atmosphere and share your values and successes with people by whom you might feel judged. A key to success is turning problems into opportunities. When faced with a misunderstanding, don't panic. Instead, use the occasion to compare and understand different points of view. This is the only way to find a common and shared solution.

Suit of Swords

Four of Swords

Solitude

Prisoner of the mind

Description: A girl with long black hair sits curled up on the floor, with her knees close to her chest. She is wearing an orange top and jeans and is barefoot. Around her is a glass bell, symbol of her inability to communicate with the environment in which she lives.

Keywords: Conservatism; practical spirit; not practicing what you preach.

Interpretation: If you can't hold back on negative criticism of colleagues, superiors, friends, or your partner, you have to understand that you are judging yourself first. You run the risk of feeding negative energies without understanding the origins of their motivations. Others, feeling unappreciated, might end relations. Try, rather, to ask yourself as an outside observer, "what do I really dislike about that person?" Answering objectively will help you, at least for a moment, to suspend judgment.

Five of Swords

Loss

Cynical or hypocritical political opinions

Description: A yellow arrow on a blue background zigzags briefly then points menacingly downward. In this case the usual interpretation of the arrow as an indicator of direction or choice is inadequate. The implicit threat here represents a discrepancy between material and spiritual values, or the religious or ideological dogma that opposes personal growth. A new course may be needed.

Keywords: Specialization, higher education; new ways of seeing the world; opponents in the workplace.

Interpretation: Maybe you are going through a period in which you are tormented and dissatisfied because of toxic relationships or environments. Until you identify the root causes that motivated you to connect with them, you will make the same mistakes. If you want to break this spiral of pain, take care of your weaknesses. Ask yourself, or explain to others, why you feel uncomfortable. This will help both you and others to understand where you are making mistakes, creating new groundwork for a more authentic relationship.

Six of Swords

Caution

Beware of reckless behavior

Description: Two men and a woman are holding up a safety net, keeping their gaze upward as if waiting to see someone or something fall. The net is connected to the sense of morality and in myth this is compared to the constellations, which symbolize the net pitched upon us from the sky to keep us from leaving the universe.

Keywords: Need to evolve or take a new road; reflective spirit, refined thoughts; intellectual narcissism.

Interpretation: You may not believe this, but if you are in a crisis you can seize unexpected opportunities and regain your balance. This is because losing your way means you held onto a dream entangled in the past. In order to change, you have to leave behind that twilight world of the unchanging past if you want to reach genuine harmony between intention and action. So banish self-pity. Instead, meet rather with friends and family to evaluate different opportunities and set new objectives.

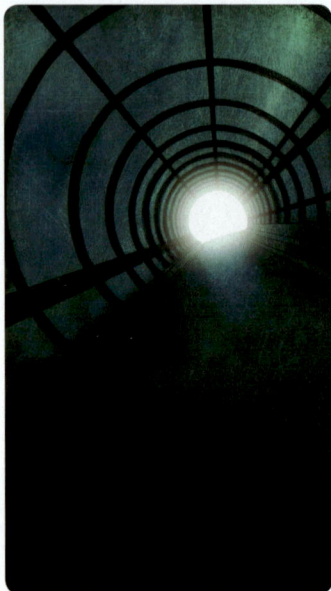

Seven of Swords

Hope

Ability to be unselfish in order to give one's best

Description: Hope is represented by a long tunnel, a direct representation of the experience of birth, when we passed from the womb to the outside world. The light indicates that it's possible to return to a normal life after all.

Keywords: Anxiety pushes us to try new paths; sage who puts own science in service of humanity, or enlightened leader; slander.

Interpretation: Your world is made up of both possibilities and limitations. To find out which are the limits you impose upon yourself, focus your attention on your thoughts that include the words "should," "need," or "it's necessary." When you notice those sentences, repeat them and ask yourself, "otherwise what happens?" If you become aware of the situation you can choose whether to keep the limitation or accept another opportunity.

Eight of Swords

Crisis

Intellectual block

Description: A young blonde woman walks unprotected down a street during a violent storm that signifies an outburst of emotions and desires, or someone who slows down our plans or interferes with our peace of mind. The ground is full of puddles, while the sky is full of dense, menacing clouds, swollen with rain.

Keywords: Delay, obstruction; positive in a spiritual sense, but creating a state of tension with the outside world; closing of a cycle.

Interpretation: The biggest waste of energy occurs when you don't connect with your experiences or people in your life. Then life can become tiresome and filled with suffering. But if you abandon your fretful efforts, which just make you feel worse, and move on with an open mind, a calm demeanor, and a relaxed attitude, everything becomes easier. Try to redirect the flow of your emotions, passing from a state of separation to a state of union with the world around you.

Nine of Swords

Mortification

Fear of losing one's individuality

Description: A tall large man, who clearly thinks very highly of himself, laughs with gusto while pointing his finger at a dejected looking man who stands beside him. This unfortunate man is a symbol of crippling shyness and the inability to assert oneself. But the card warns: it does not help to feel inferior.

Keywords: The past is called into question; listening and being open toward a thought free of criticism and comparisons; crises, depression, unhappiness.

Interpretation: We all have the power to increase the quality of our own life because we create our world with our choices. If our present does not satisfy us, often it is because we haven't the courage to change. Take your existence into your own hands and take a stand. Resolve to stop postponing that which needs to be decided here and now. Train your mind and your heart with a strategy for success. Transform your problems into an opportunity for growth.

Ten of Swords

Defeat

Possible quarrels and in-gratitude

Description: The card shows a shipwreck, representing a stage of existential dejection where we must move cautiously, facing a period in which everything is topsy-turvy. For Jung, however, the sinking ship represents renewed and regained energies which result from a critical period and that help us aim for new horizons.

Keywords: Higher mental maturity; acceptance of a differing point of view; find the cause of one's troubles and fight it tenaciously.

Interpretation: If you want to overcome the crisis that is crippling you, see if you can recognize the phase you are experiencing. How are you facing its challenges and seizing its opportunities? Are you able to think "beyond yourself" and convince yourself that only by giving to others do you really receive? The conclusions you come to will help you reach that decision-making moment made up of inner clarity, allowing you to realize your goals.

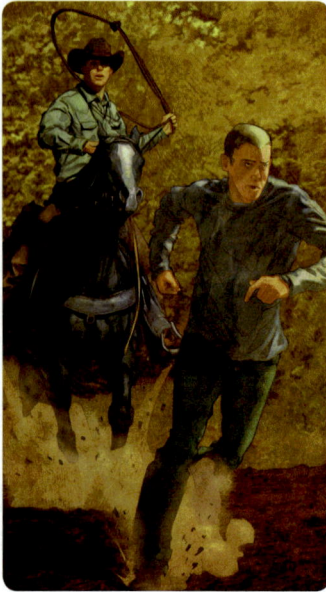

Knave of Swords

The guardian

Prudence and perseverance

Description: On a country road a youth in cowboy attire is trying to catch and restrain another boy running ahead of him. It is an image that evokes social or emotional obligations - both sought after and refused. Our feelings are often contradictory due to our richly nuanced personality. However, when it comes time to choose, it's best to opt for a precise path.

Keywords: Lack of confidence; attempt to discover which path to follow; falsehood, underestimation, intellectual confusion.

Interpretation: Unfortunately you can't seem to live with passion or conviction. It is as if you've frozen a vital part of yourself as a means of self-protection. If you can't decide instantly what makes you more alive, you can start by taking stock of past experiences, considering that which brought you the most joy. What would you have liked? A child? A new career? Keep visualizing these choices, paying attention to the emotions they spark and to the sensations in your body.

Knight of Swords

The fighter

Solution to a problem

Description: a man wearing pants, a shirt, and tie carries a shield – a weapon that defends us from the negative side of life – slipped under his arm. In one hand he grasps a sword, symbol of the intellect which separates the useful from the useless, good from bad. It is also a symbol of true creative, active, and vital energy. His face wears the expression of someone preparing to wage a tough battle.

Keywords: Courage, experience and cunning; fight for a spiritual cause to be transmitted to the whole world; depending on the circumstances, the fighter can be an enemy or a champion.

Interpretation: Whether you are defending your own interests or those of others, you always trust your intuition and emotions without getting bogged down in long discussions or detailed plans. This is because you are not calculating. Often, however, you find yourself having to diffuse tensions you unwittingly created in the heat of the moment. Try to think about how you act. Ask yourself if your attitude might hurt someone. This way you can avoid having to mend things in the future.

Queen of Swords

The rival

Vindictive Intelligence

Description: Two women are portrayed trying to pull a rope, revealing a clear refusal to enter adulthood, but also an almost inescapable and not always pleasant bond that unites people capable of defending their views obstinately. One of the women has a severe look and clearly knows how to defend herself only by attacking.

Keywords: Rejection of the body; rationalism taken to extremes; solitude, widowhood or divorce.

Interpretation: In order to keep passion alive, sexuality needs variety, experimentation, and continuous involvement. During intimacy, use body language to communicate with each other so as to avoid misunderstanding and incomprehension: play between the sheets, have fun with caresses and different positions, give free expression to your imagination and fantasies, playing different roles. You will nourish the enjoyment of discovery of yourself and your partner.

Suit of Swords

King of Swords

The professor

Obeying the rules and laws

Description: A man dressed in an elegant but basic manner has an air of someone knows how to assume responsibility with firmness and decisiveness. He personifies the rigor and obedience of rules and laws, but he also knows how to use the authority conferred upon him by his family or community. He may be single, widowed, or separated, or someone who treats his work as if it were a mission and he does not want to have emotional commitments that might distract him.

Keywords: Wisdom, justice, incorruptibility; coldness in love; risk of insensitivity or lack of respect for the feelings of others.

Interpretation: You generally face life with the strength of a lion, king of the forest and animals. Perhaps, however, the commanding role has put you at risk of being the target of other people's problems. Shed some light on what is behind your personal belief system. You might discover whether those around you share it or if it is time to become more autonomous and independent. Be aware that in any case you will never be able to make everyone happy, unless you are untrue to yourself and those around you.

Spreads

Now that you know the cards in the Law of Attraction Tarot, it's time to learn how to use them. The spreads that follow may help you to learn more about yourself and your desires. Keep in mind that the real purpose of the Tarot is understanding oneself rather than predicting the future, and that the "future" is only one of many possible developments of our present.

Nothing happens by chance, and the first thing to do is to better understand why we foster a certain desire. Together, these Tarot cards are an effective tool for doing so, as they help us reach a state of deep concentration where time dissolves and everything becomes clear. On a practical level, you can help your mind with small rituals: for example, before a reading you can relax, quieting both your mind and your body, and focusing on an image that inspires positive feelings in you (a flame, the sea, the sky). Before starting a spread, depending on your values and your religious beliefs, you can also say a small prayer of thanks.

Make sure that every part of you is in harmony.

On a practical level

Keeping them face down, choose from the Tarot deck the number of cards required by the spread of your choice and arrange them as described. Each card will give you a hint.

Turn the cards over, one by one, consult their meaning and listen to what they have to tell you.

The Celtic Cross
To get a clearer idea of what we want

This spread can be used to answer a question regarding a desire we've been considering for a while as well as to better understand its characteristics.

After shuffling the 22 Major Arcana, have the querent cut the deck. The choice of only Major Arcana is recommended for beginners, while more experienced readers can use the whole deck. Reassemble the deck, then begin to arrange the cards in the sequence indicated, saying as you take each card, the following phrases:

1. This card is your current wish.
2. This card influences your wish.
3. This card is its goal.
4. This card represents the motivations that generated it.
5. This card represents future influences that will act upon it.
6. This card concerns your current state.
7. This card concerns your greatest strength in putting it in to practice.
8. This card concerns your hopes and fears regarding your wish.
9. This card concerns the obstacles you may encounter.
10. This card concerns its final outcome.

The Astromantic Wheel
To get an overview of your desire.

This Spread makes use the complete Tarot deck, but uses the 22 Major Arcana and the 56 Minor Arcana separately.

You can use this spread when you do not want to ask a specific question, but rather get an overall view of the general situation of your wish and verifying its actual conditions. Each card drawn represents one facet.

This spread is complete and fairly complex. It draws on astrological techniques, so those who already have some knowledge of this discipline will find it easier.

Once you have shuffled the Major Arcana, the querent must draw twelve cards, which are then arranged counterclockwise in the form of a wheel. Those familiar with astrology will recognize the positions of the natal chart. Each position is called a House and refers to a facet of the desire in question. The position of the Ascendant is the first House, the remaining eleven follow in order.

Meanings of the twelve Houses:
1st House: your desire and its possibilities of realization
2nd House: good or bad use of money that affect the goal. Debts and credits you may contract.
3rd House: contacts, studies, and short trips that may be useful. The attitude of your siblings vis-a-vis your wish.
4th House: help your immediate family may be able to give.
5th House: how to use creativity in all its forms to realize your wish.
6th House: the effort you are willing to put in, day after day, to see your dream come true.
7th House: your willingness to associate or collaborate with someone. The importance of interpersonal relationships in getting what you want.

8th House: possibility of finding investors if your desire consists of a project or innovative idea, but also possible inheritances that can help you raise the funds you need.

9th House: relations with distant places and persons may provide valuable suggestions or providential help. Your desire may require you to relocate or travel abroad.

10th House: the culmination of the efforts you've made to see your wish fulfilled. Official recognition of your talent.

11th House: the friendships, affinities, protection, and help you could receive. Everything that takes place before an audience.

12th House: the House which reconnects to the first. It is the epilogue, the conclusion of all told by the previous eleven Houses.

After this first reading of the Major Arcana, we proceed to develop the spread by extracting from the deck of Minor Arcana one or more cards, up to a maximum of three for each House in which you want to delve further into interpretation, discovering the relevant details.

Example

The querent is 29 years old, has a degree in industrial design due to good grades, willpower, and initiative, but has not yet found a professional position in line with her major. Recently she has resorted to performing various types of work just to make ends meet, but would now like to enroll in a massage course to get certified so she can work independently. The course is expensive, and her parents are willing to help pay for part of it in order to see her settled.

The cards were extracted in the following order:
(see layout on page 146)
1st House: XI – Self confidence
2nd House: IV – Inner maturity
3rd House: VII – Dynamism
4th House: V – Coherence
5th House: XXI – The Accomplishment
6th House: III – The Formulation
7th House: 0 – Confusion
8th House: XIII – Il Change
9th House: XIV – Reflection
10th House: I – Planning
11th House: IX – Concentration
12th House: XVII – Optimism

In the 1st House, Self Confidence tells us that the time is right for the querent to undertake something new and that the chances of realizing her desire are excellent, as long as she believes in what she is doing.

In the **2nd House**, which corresponds to money necessary to fulfill her desire, is **Inner Maturity**. This is an invitation to think twice before spending the money required, to consult a reliable person regarding the effective validity of the course she wishes to attend.

In the **3rd House** we find **Dynamism**. This concerns contacts, studies and/or small trips essential to attaining her wish. This card indicates the need to be very flexible about the time and place of the course. The querent must evaluate her current commitments and ask herself if she can manage everything.

In the **4th House**, which refers to help that her original family could give her, the **Coherence** card indicates a quite helpful father, provided she is willing to follow his suggestions.

In the 5th House is Accomplishment. It means the possibility of attending this course is making the querent forget her past, pushing her to project and plan how she might pursue her work once she gets her certification as a masseuse.

In the 6th House the card of Formulation indicates the need to always find the right words to face rules, duties, and commitments that the course requires, in the best and most effective manner.

In the 7th House, Confusion means that friends may not always be on the querent's side with regard to this decision. But she will be determined to follow her own path and will continue to cultivate her own desire.

In the 8th House, which is about money, the Change card underlines the end of a phase of her life in which she did not have a secure income, followed by another in which the querent could have a more prosperous and secure financial situation.

Reflection in the 9th House, that of distance, indicates that the querent may need to compromise on how and where she will run her own business, whilst trying to be true to herself and her environment.

Planning in the 10th House, that of the realization of the ego, says that only if she has clear ideas will she obtain the professional renewal she wishes for, canceling out all resistance from other people and situations.

In the 11th House the card of Concentration calls on her to not fall prey to discouragement if sometimes things don't work as she would like them to. Control and moderation must be her rallying cry.

In the 12th House, the Optimism indicates that because of this course the querent could finally carve out her own space in the professional realm.

For a final confirmation that the path chosen is the right one, let's take a look at the Minor Arcana for a final verdict.

The querent's question is: "Should I sign up for this professional course?" She chooses three cards from the deck of Minor Arcana.

The cards are:

The Worker = searching for one's place in the world

The Fighter = solution to a problem.

Spirit of Initiative = necessary determination to accomplish one's wish.

The decision to enroll in this course therefore seems appropriate, provided the querent can demonstrate a high level of confidence in her own abilities and a good dose of fighting spirit to succeed, taking strength from the innate conviction that she is doing the right thing.

The Fish
To improve intentional attraction

A legend says that fish know everything since they are in contact with primitive, vital, and regenerative forces, but they are silent. It takes magic to "make them talk."

With this layout the querent will become aware of any negative vibrations, usually in the form of doubts, that hinder the manifestation of his/her desire.

To do the Spread of the Fish, you need to shuffle the deck (or only the Major Arcana cards if the reader is a novice) and randomly choose nine cards, then lay them out according to the layout.

Cards 1, 2, and 3 represent all that has to do with past circumstances that have shaped and influenced the querent's desire.

Card 1, that which the querent has repressed and would scare him/her should the dream come true.

Card 2, the memories that haunt the querent and which s/he cannot escape.

Card 3 ways the querent can break free from the past and move forward; it represents a sort of meditation.

Cards 4,5 and 6 are the querent's present.

Card 4 is the emotional aspect of his or her present: emotions, hopes, and fears regarding his or her wish.

Card 5 is the practical aspect: what needs to be done for the wish to come true.

Card 6 clarifies the querent's spiritual needs: what s/he needs to do in order to live his/her dream on a more conscious level.

Cards 7,8 and 9 are the future.

Card 7 provides insight: the best way for the subject to act in the immediate future to get closer to his/her wish.

Card 8 is magic: it reveals how to propitiate the wish and make it come true as the subject would like it to.

Card 9 is the final answer: it clarifies what will occur and if outcome will bring happiness.

The Crab

To understand the origins of limiting beliefs

This spread can help the querent understand how his or her limiting beliefs have negatively influenced the manifestation of their wish. The Crab grabs the future with its claws, but everything is connected in harmony to the present and the past.

If there are delays in making progress it is because a ring is missing. Maybe the querent is not aware of the obstacles that hinder his or her goals, or he or she does not want to be responsible for it.

To get a better idea, the querent can shuffle the deck, and draw six cards one by one and put them down according to the layout.

Cards 1 and 2 represent the past: The 1st, his or her inner feelings that led certain choices regarding achieving the wish; the 2nd, the influenced events affecting his or her actions.

Cards 3 and 4 are the present: the 3rd is how the querent feels right now, both fears and hopes; the 4th is the external reality, those conditions that influences the querent.

Cards 5 and 6 are the future of his or her desire: the 5th represents that which he or she hopes or fears about the future; the 6th is what will really happen.

The Seagull

To understand if we are allowing our wish to come true.

Here is a spread that can allow the querent to fly towards a higher awareness. Looking at things from above, you can see the bigger picture and notice whether you are, on a subconscious level, implementing strategies that are preventing the manifestation of your wish. It is above all a spread for discovering if the desire you are cultivating is really yours or if it based on the expectations of people around you.

In any case the seagull frees its energies capable of working in a more targeted manner to obtain what is desired. In addition, there are seven cards in this spread; the number seven is traditionally considered to be a very powerful and magical number.

The querent must shuffle the deck, then draw seven cards and lay them out according to the figure below:

Card 1 is the querent, mainly how s/he lives this wish, which emotions are experienced and which attitudes are exhibited.

Card 2 is the wish, with its positive and negative sides, made of hopes and contradictions.

Card 3 indicates what s/he wants more than anything from this wish, even if s/he is unable to admit it; this reveals the secret power, the "ace in the hole" that makes this wish unique and different from all the rest.

Card 4 is what the desire wants from s/he who created and nourished it, in other words, what is demanded from the querent.

Card 5 represents the obstacles and difficulties of this wish, the knots the querent keeps inside.

Card 6 are the obstacles and difficulties from the wish's perspective. These may not coincide with the problems of the querent.

Card 7 is the final answer regarding the desire in question, what kind of energy it makes with its creator, the characteristics they form together.

The Three-card Method
To know and effectively manage one's wish

In this spread you can use both the Major Arcana as well as the Minor Arcana, keeping them separated.

From the 22 Major Arcana, the querent chooses three cards and lays them out in a triangle according to the figure in the positions marked by roman numerals.

The querent must draw four cards from the Minor Arcana and place them in the cardinal points marked in Arabic numerals.

The Three Card Method can be easily learned and mastered. It is particularly suited for going forward with the utmost conviction toward one's wish and discovering ahead of time any unexpected challenges or situations so they can be faced appropriately.

The first three Major Arcana represent:
I – The prospect of the desire in the present
II – Its development
III – Its conclusion

The Minor Arcana cards provide further details of great importance to further understand the desire providing a link between each of the Major Arcana.

1 – the link between the present and its development
2 – the link between the development and the conclusion
3 – the link between the present and the conclusion
4 – the link between the present, its development and the conclusion

The Judge's Spread
To learn to wish in a positive manner

This spread with its unusual name is one of the most effective ones for getting an answer in case of doubt, as it helps address every aspect of life – love, work, leisure – with a winning attitude, helping to achieve what you dream and what you want. After the querent draws 4 cards (you can use just the Major Arcana if you want a simpler reading), they should be positioned according to the layout.

1. In favor
2. Against
3. The Judge
4. The Judgment

The first card "in favor" indicates everything which benefits the achievement of the desire; the second card, "Against" warns of the dangers one may meet along the way; the third card above "The Judge" is the decision – that which must be done to make it a reality; the fourth card below, "The Judgment" will give the definitive answer, therefore indicating whether the desire will be achieved or not.

Conclusion

A brief note from the author

*I have been asked why I felt the need
to create this Tarot deck.*

*It is a difficult question.
I can only say that I created these cards
because I believe that only by realizing
our most authentic dreams can
we truly be happy.*

*These Tarot cards want to help
whoever consults them to achieve a leap in ability,
to go from carrying out approximate actions
and choices that might be dictated
by the expectations or pressures of others,
to authentic actions and choices,
decided upon autonomously,
driving forward with more conviction
towards self-realization.*

Good luck!

Marina